Jacques Choron is a distinguished philosopher and long-time student of self-destructive phenomena. Most recently he has been a Fellow at the Suicide Prevention Center in Los Angeles, California, and a Fellow at the center for Studies of Suicide Prevention at the National Institute of Mental Health, Rockville, Maryland. He is the author of *Death and Western Thought* and *Modern Man and Mortality,* among other books.

SUICIDE

JACQUES CHORON

SUICIDE

Charles Scribner's Sons • New York

Copyright © 1972 Jacques Choron

The research for this book was supported by Public Health Service grants
MH 38615-01 and -02 from the National Institute of Mental Health.

This book published simultaneously in the United States of America and in Canada
—Copyright under the Berne Convention

All rights reserved. No part of this book may be reproduced in any form without the
permission of Charles Scribner's Sons.

A-1.72(V)

Printed in the United States of America
Library of Congress Catalog Card Number 75-162757
SBN 684-12577-3

To my sister Fenia

Contents

	Introduction	3
1	Suicide in Retrospect	9
2	Facts and Figures	34
3	Methods of Suicide	38
4	Attempted Suicide	43
5	Suicide among Adolescents	51
6	The Search for Causes	56
7	Suicide and Mental Disorders	74
8	Suicide Prevention	79
9	The Psychological Autopsy	86
10	Terms and Definitions	91
11	The Problem of "Rational Suicide"	96
12	The Problem of "Easy Dying"	102
13	Philosophers on Suicide	107
14	Suicide and the Meaning of Life	139
	Conclusion: Suicide in Perspective	152
	Appendix: Assessment of Suicidal Potential	159
	Reference Notes	163
	Index	177

SUICIDE

INTRODUCTION

Ever since man's self-awareness and its corollary, the awareness of his mortality, have made him capable of taking his own life, suicide has been the object of dread as well as of curiosity far exceeding that directed toward any other manner of death.

At the dawn of history, anything connected with death had special importance, and the dead were frightening and "unclean" (taboo). This feeling was even stranger toward those whom the early Greeks called *biaiothanatoi*—people who died, by violence or otherwise, before their time. But, even among these, suicides occupied a special place. To have acted as they did, they must have been greatly wronged in some way; therefore their ghosts were unusually revengeful and dangerous. One may wonder how much of this primitive fear, rooted in "magical" thought and guilt feelings is still awakened whenever someone we know, no matter how slightly, commits suicide.

But there are other, more obvious reasons which make people feel uneasy, fearful, or angry, when confronted with a suicide. The religious man who believes that everyone's life belongs to God resents the suicide's interference with the divine plan. The secularized man objects to suicide as being "against nature." Even those who recognize only "his majesty chance" believe that the contingency of birth ought to extend also to death and that therefore the individual should not interfere with "chance" in this respect either.

Moreover, it is easier for people to reconcile themselves to death when it comes as if decreed by destiny. This aspect of suicide is beautifully expressed by the Roman statesman, Pliny the Younger (62?-c. 113):

> Corellius Rufus has died, and died by his own wish, which makes me even sadder; for death is most tragic when it is not due to fate or natural causes. When we see men die of disease, at least we can find consolation in the knowledge that it is inevitable, but, when their end is self-sought, our grief is inconsolable because we feel that their lives could have been long.[1]

It has been suggested that suicide "troubles and appalls us because it so intransigently rejects our deeply held conviction that life must be worth living."[2]

While there is undoubtedly some truth in this, in more cases than one would like to admit the reason for the shock may not be the challenges to the belief that life is good, but the fact that one is not really quite sure that it is. As the modern Spanish philosopher José Ortega y Gasset has pointed out, for most people at all times "life" meant limitation, obligation, dependence, and oppression. They go on living simply because they happen to have been born, sustained by the force of habit, sometimes out of curiosity or vague hopes for a better future, and because they are afraid of the alternative —death.[3] But the suicide seems to have conquered this fear. Thus he confirms not only the suspicion that life may not be the highest good but the one that death may not be the greatest evil. In challenging the usual attitudes toward both life and death, the suicide is not merely a nonconformist but also a seducer, and this is one of the reasons that most civilized societies consider him almost as dangerous as he appeared to primitive man when his unappeased ghost was thought to threaten the welfare of the tribe.

This accounts for the strict condemnation of suicide in

Introduction

most cultures. However, people did commit suicide, sometimes for motives that were laudable, or at least under circumstances that were understandable. The indiscriminate condemnation had to admit some exceptions. Moreover, with growing sophistication, intermittent "failure of nerve," and spreading philosophical reflection on life and death, man's ability to take his own life began to appear in a different light. Some even saw it as a great boon, a precious privilege. The only real questions were under what circumstances this privilege might be exercised, or what exceptions could be tolerated. When was suicide good and when was it evil? When was it right and when wrong? From classical antiquity until the nineteenth century all thought and writing on suicide were dominated by this issue. In other words, suicide was treated as a religio-ethical and legal problem.

By comparison with suicide as a problem, the problem of suicide—that is, the question of why some people kill themselves while most others in similar circumstances do not—came to the fore much later. This does not mean that some, even among the ancients, did not seek an explanation other than that given by the suicides themselves. The connection between melancholia and suicide goes back to Hippocrates, and to Galen's theory of the four humors. The search for the real causes of suicide was resumed as soon as it became possible to see it not exclusively, as Christianity did, in terms of sin and the Devil's work. Burton's *Anatomy of Melancholy* (1628), Jean Dumas' *Traité du suicide ou du meurtre volontaire* (1773), Esquirol's *Sur la monomanie suicide* (1827), Bourdin's *Du suicide considéré comme maladie* (1845), and Brierre de Boismont's *Du suicide et de la folie suicide* (1856) represent the most important efforts to explain suicidal behavior as resulting from mental disorders. In the last third of the nineteenth century students of society also turned their attention toward suicide. The basis of their investigations was the gradually accumulated statistics on suicide, and the motive of their studies was the desire to discover "laws" in the seemingly capricious human behavior similar to the laws of nature. The relatively stable suicide rates in a given society which the statistics made apparent were assumed to result from extra-individual (social) forces. This was the thesis defended by Enrico Morselli in his *Il suicido* (1879). In the same year Thomas Masaryk, the future founder of the Czechoslovak Republic, then a candidate for a chair at the University of Vienna, submitted a dissertation, *Suicide as a Social Mass-Phenomenon (Selbstmord als soziale Massenerscheinung,* published in 1881), in which, under the false impression that suicide does not occur in primitive societies, he maintained that the increase in the incidence of suicide was due to modern civilization and the decline of religion. Toward the end of the century, in 1897, appeared Emile Durkheim's *Le Suicide,* the basic sociological study of suicide. None of the works mentioned in this paragraph, however, was morally neutral, and the suicide statistics underlying them went under the name of "moral statistics." It is only in the twentieth century that moral bias was completely eliminated from scientific—psychiatric or sociological—studies of suicide. And it is only since the mid-1950s that any unprecedented upsurge of interest in suicidal phenomena has taken place, not only among psychiatrists but also among psychologists, sociologists, and anthropologists.

This fact is reflected in the number of titles—over 1200—for the period 1957-1967, in *Bibliography on Suicide and Suicide Prevention* compiled by Norman L. Farberow (1969). This bibliography contains close to 3400 items, from 1897 through 1967. A bibliography by Hans Rost published in 1927 contains approximately 3800. There is some overlapping between the two bibliographies, but it can be safely assumed that the total of books and articles on suicide exceeds 7000. The change of emphasis from suicide as a problem to the problem of suicide is dramatically illustrated by the fact that in the bibliography included in *The Cry for Help,* edited by Farberow and Edwin S. Shneidman, which

Introduction

contains approximately 2100 items (1897 through 1957) only 25 were listed under "Religious-Philosophical," the rest being categorized as "Psychological-General," "Sociological," and "Medical-Legal."[4]

While the quantity of literature on suicide in the past decade is impressive, its quality leaves much to be desired. According to M. J. Kahne, who made a survey of recent medical suicide literature, "the monotonous regularity with which the same types of data are reported and the same stereotyped conclusions inferred from information organized in a fashion whose methodological error has long since been demonstrated is only too rarely broken by original ventures beyond the conventional. Indeed most of the literature does not even qualify as research."[5] David Lester in his detailed review of research findings concurs in this unfavorable appraisal.[6]

One explanation for the sudden interest in suicide in the past fifteen years was certainly the growing realization that the number of suicides was high enough to present a serious challenge to those concerned with social well-being and mental health, a fact to which, in the United States, Louis Dublin called attention as early as 1933 in his book *To Be or Not to Be*.[7] However, a significant role was also played by the almost simultaneous discovery in England and the United States that several times as many people attempt suicide as succeed in carrying it out and that an attempt at suicide is essentially a "cry for help." That is, most people who try to kill themselves are ambivalent about it; what they really want is not to die but merely to achieve a change in the conditions of their existence. Finally, suicide, from the psychoanalytical perspective, appeared as the last stage of a general aggressive and destructive tendency in man. It would be surprising if the heightened concern with suicide did not also reflect the spiritual crisis of our times, with its questioning of traditional values, and no matter how indirectly, the search for an affirmative answer to the question of life's worth and meaning.

1

SUICIDE IN RETROSPECT

Suicide in Primitive Cultures

Until late into the nineteenth century suicide was not believed to occur among primitives. This view was decisively influenced by the notion of the "happy savage" promulgated by the French philosopher Jean-Jacques Rousseau (1712-1778) and the belief in the Golden Age which was supposed to have reigned at the dawn of history. Obviously, no cause for suicide could exist under paradisiacal conditions, or among happy people. Rousseau's contemporary, Voltaire, held that "savages did not consider killing themselves out of disgust for life: this is a refinement of civilized man *(gens d'ésprit)*."[1]

Anthropological studies have since refuted the contention that primitives do not commit suicide. In 1896 the German sociologist Alfred Vierkandt reported mass suicides on Madagascar and in New Zealand,[2] and later studies have revealed that suicide took place in primitive societies all over the world and that in some of them the rate was quite high, especially among women.

The anthropologist Edward Westermark (1862-1939) gives the various motives which led primitives to kill themselves: "Disappointed love or jealousy; illness or old age; grief over the death of a child, husband or wife; fear of punishment; slavery or brutal treatment by a husband; remorse, shame or wounded pride; anger or revenge. In various cases the offended person kills himself for the express purpose of taking revenge on the offender—'killing oneself upon the head of another'."[3]

Nevertheless, the view that suicide did not exist among primitives is not entirely wrong if degrees of primitiveness are taken into account, even though the reasons for its absence among our truly primitive ancestors are not those assumed in the idealized view of their condition. Obviously, suicide was impossible until man discovered certain things about death and also about himself, and this knowledge was acquired only very gradually, and relatively late in the long prehistory of the human species. Even though the "complete" discovery of death as a natural and inevitable event was not a necessary precondition of suicide, the most primitive notion of death as due exclusively to the influence of malignant magical forces had to be overcome or at least enlarged by the knowledge that one could be killed by wild beasts or other men, and that one could also inflict death on others. Obviously, the latter had to include some information about the particularly vulnerable parts of human anatomy, which presupposes a certain degree of sophistication. In this connection a passage in the Talmud concerning the slaying of Abel is of interest. The rabbis realized that the first murderer would be ignorant about the ways of achieving his goal. They therefore expand on the biblical tale by suggesting that Cain hit his brother repeatedly, inflicting numerous bruises and wounds, none of which was fatal. Finally, he struck him in the neck "where the soul abideth" and thus caused his death.

Still, there is a considerable difference between killing

another human being and killing oneself. I do not refer here to the psychological difference (emotional and motivational) which I discuss in another context, nor to the difference in methods; since primitive man's techniques for killing an adversary are not easily applicable to committing suicide. It is idle to speculate about the method of the earliest suicides. Considering the almost universal "pull" exercised by high places, jumping to one's death may well have been the first and most "natural" way.

The second development necessary to make suicide possible was man's growing consciousness of himself as an individual. This was totally absent, or at least little developed, when man was aware of himself primarily as an integral part of the clan. The awakening of self-consciousness allowed him to see himself, as it were, from the outside. It is therefore justifiable to assert that the "primitive" societies in which suicide does take place are already relatively "advanced."

If this view of the preconditions for suicide is correct, it automatically excludes the possibility of suicide among animals, and all the stories asserting the contrary should be dismissed as myths. The behavior of lemmings in periodically rushing into the sea, for example, should not be assumed to be suicide. But what about the faithful dogs who are said to starve themselves to death on the graves of their masters? In considering such reports, one must allow for the anthropomorphic interpretations of canine behavior to which dog lovers are well known to be addicted.

The matter becomes more complicated, however, if one admits the possibility that animals know of death. As far as the knowledge of death in animals is concerned, there is no evidence for it and the experiments devised by Halmuth Schaefer do not seem to be conclusive or even properly conceived.[4] And before one allows that self-destruction does occur among higher animals, one may ask why there are no more reports of animal suicides from farmers, animal breeders, and zoologists, especially in view of the innumerable occasions to observe such behavior.

SUICIDE

The Early Egyptians

But to return to man. The first known document dealing with suicide is an ancient Egyptian text known as "The Dialogue of a Misanthrope with His Own Soul" or simply as "Dispute over Suicide."[5] A man tired of life because of a series of misfortunes and contemplating suicide wants to convince his soul to accompany him into death, but the soul hesitates because it is afraid that in committing suicide the man will be deprived of a proper funeral and thus forsake the soul's chances of a blissful afterlife. It tries therefore to induce him to abandon his project and to turn instead to a life of hedonistic pleasures. This the man refuses to do because life has no rewards to offer, and particularly because a life of indulgence would bring his name into "evil odor."

The misanthrope of the dialogue emerges as a decent person unable to adjust to the violence and injustice of his times and the dog-eat-dog morality, as evidenced by the second of the four poems of the text:

> To whom can I speak today?
> [One's] fellows are evil;
> The friends of today do not love . . .
> Hearts are rapacious:
> Every man seizes his fellow's goods . . .
> The gentle man has perished,
> [But] the violent man has access to everybody . . .
> There are no righteous;
> The land is left to those who do wrong . . .
> To whom can I speak today? I am laden with
>   wretchedness
> For lack of intimate friends. . . .

In this work social isolation and loneliness emerge as the main reason for contemplating suicide. It is interesting that the prominent role of loneliness in the causation of suicide has been recently emphasized by several students. Because of it death becomes irresistibly attractive:

> Death is in my sight today
> Like the recovery of a sick man . . .
> Like the longing of a man to see his house again
> After many years of captivity . . . .

But death is attractive also because it leads to another existence in which justice prevails and the dead share divine privileges:

> Why surely, he who is yonder,
> shall seize [the culprit] like a living god
> . . . He shall stand in the celestial bark. . . .

The Ancient Hebrews

Since belief in a happy afterlife is clearly suicide-promoting, it may be partly because the Old Testament contains no promise of immortality that one finds only six suicides recorded there. They are Abimelech (Judges 9:54), Samson (Judges 16:28-31), Saul (I Samuel 31:1-6), Saul's armor bearer (Chronicles 10), Achitophel (II Samuel 17:23), and Zimri (I Kings 16:9). However, the infrequency of suicide among the Jews of the Old Testament period was more a result of their strong attachment to life and their positive attitude toward the world. "God saw everything that he had made, and, behold, it was very good." (Genesis I:30). If God finds his work satisfactory, who is man to find fault with it? An even more important factor was their limitless trust in God's wisdom and justice and his care for his people. In spite of all Job's suffering, he resisted the temptation of suicide (Job 2:9-10). For these reasons those who did commit suicide were considered insane or at least temporarily deranged, and no sanctions were taken against suicides. Their bodies were not desecrated, and they were not refused the usual funeral rites.

Despite the infrequency of suicide among the Hebrews one of the most spectacular mass suicides of ancient times occurred among them. It is probably significant that this happened in A.D. 74, after the destruction of the second Temple by the Romans and at a time when the belief in a hereafter, proclaimed by the sect of Pharisees, had become widespread. All the members of the garrison of the fortress of Massada, together with their women and children, chose death in preference to captivity. Massada was the last stronghold of the Zealots to hold out against the overpowering might of the Roman legions of Titus. The Jewish historian Josephus Flavius, a former general who, after being defeated, surrendered to the Romans and became an intimate of Titus, relates what happened. Realizing that further resistance was useless, the commander of Massada, Eleazar, reminded his troops of their original resolve never to become slaves of the Romans and called on them to die by their own hand. When they hesitated he added another argument—namely that "death affords our souls their liberty and sends them to their own place of purity, where they are to be insensible to all sorts of miseries." Whereupon his soldiers killed their wives and children; some committed suicide; and others drew lots to determine which one should kill his companions and then die by his own hand. When the Romans stormed the fortress they found only two women and five children who hid in a cave and escaped the massacre. It is they who related the events recorded by Josephus.

It is interesting that some years prior to these events Josephus found himself in similar circumstances when he was commanding a detachment of Jewish troops which was surrounded by the Romans. On that occasion the soldiers wanted to kill themselves rather than become slaves, and Josephus tried to prevent a mass suicide, arguing that it was "a wicked and perfidious act to cast out of one's body the soul which God has committed to it." His plea fell on deaf ears. He was accused of cowardice and threatened with death. According to his own account, in order to save his own life he proposed that "they commit mutual slaughter by lot," to which they agreed. "By chance or by the providence of God" he and one soldier remained as the last survivors, and Josephus persuaded his companion to surrender to the Romans.[6] It is difficult to admire Josephus's behavior; his only excuse is that he might have been sincere in his argument against suicide.

The Ancient Greeks

The Greeks of the Homeric period considered suicide as a "natural" and fitting solution to a variety of precarious situations. The first suicide mentioned by Homer is that of Jocasta, the mother of Oedipus. During Odysseus's visit to the Underworld he saw that unfortunate woman who in ignorance "wrought an awful deed by marrying her own son" (who equally in ignorance slew his own father) and "went to the house of Hades, fastening a high noose from the lofty hall" *(Odyssey,* XI, 271 ff.). It is not clear whether she hanged herself when she discovered the horrible truth or because of shame when the facts became known. But the narrator does not attach any blame to her for having committed suicide. Rather it appears as the only fitting act for a person in such a dreadful predicament.

More generally, when life lost all that made it worth living in the estimation of the individual concerned, suicide was considered as the only reasonable solution. Aside from the committing of a horrible crime, the most prominent among these reasons was dishonor, real or imaginary. The suicide of Ajax the Greater belongs to the latter category. Ajax, the son of Telamon, king of Salamis, and second only to Achilles in strength and bravery, rescued the latter's body from the Trojans when the arrow, shot by Paris and guided by Apollo, struck the greatest of the Greek warriors in his only vulnerable spot, his heel. But after Achilles's death his armor was not given to Ajax but to Odysseus *(Odyssey,* XL, 541). Ajax felt dishonored and, according to one version, became so enraged that his anger caused his death; another version, however, was that he slew himself.

Another well-publicized suicide in this category was that of Pantites, the lone survivor of the battle of Thermopylae (480 B.C.). On his return to Sparta he was held in dishonor and hanged himself. Incidentally, suicide by hanging was regarded by the Greeks as a shameful kind of death.

Unrequited love seems to have been an accepted reason for suicide. Famous was the suicide of Dido, the legendary founder and queen of Carthage. When Aeneas, one of the outstanding defenders of Troy, landed in Carthage on his flight from the defeated city, Dido fell in love with him, and when he deserted her, she stabbed herself.

No less important a reason for suicide was the death of a loved one. When Theseus sailed for Crete to slay the monster Minotaur he promised his father, Aegeus, that if he returned victorious he would hoist a white sail instead of the original black one. But he forgot to do so, and when Aegeus, who was anxiously awaiting the return of the ship, saw the black sail, he assumed that his son was dead. He flung himself from the rock on which he had been keeping watch and was drowned in the sea, which was thereafter called Aegean.

Perhaps even more well known was the story of the suicide of Hero, the priestess of Aphrodite at Sestos, on the Hellespont (Dardanelles). Her lover Leander who lived in Abydos on the other side of the strait swam it nightly to visit her, and Hero used to put up a light to guide him. One stormy night the wind blew out the flame, and Leander drowned. When his body was washed ashore the next morning Hero threw herself into the sea.

The suicides most highly regarded in Greek mythology as well as in Homer were the heroic suicides—the sacrifice of one's life for the benefit of another, and in particular for the defense of one's country. Such suicides were honored and admired. Society tacitly and sometimes openly encouraged them. Heroic suicides are obviously quite different from those brought on by serious illness, grief, or an unbearable situation and in this sense are outside the scope of an investigation primarily for the purpose of preventing suicide as an undesirable psycho-social phenomenon. However, Greek historians do not record many such suicides. One of the most glorious chapters in Greek history, the defense of the Thermopylae pass against the Persian army by Leonidas, king of Sparta, and his three hundred companions, can scarcely be considered an example, even though the defenders must have known that they were embarking on a suicidal mission. Two other incidents of mass suicide are also reported by the Greek historian Thucydides (c. 460-400 B.C.). Both took place at Corcyra, one in 427 B.C., the other in 425 B.C. In the first instance, fifty members of the oligarchic party were condemned to death, and all escaped execution by killing one another or hanging themselves. Two years later a considerable number of members of the same party were trapped in a building and in groups of twenty were led to execution. When the other prisoners realized the fate reserved for them they killed themselves, either by thrusting arrows into their throats or by hanging themselves.

Although the Homeric Greeks seem to have accepted suicide as the proper solution in certain circumstances, they generally held a strongly positive view of life. The only criticism leveled against it was its brevity. At the same time their view of death was anything but cheerful, as evidenced from the remark of the shade of Achilles to Odysseus, that it is better to be a slave on earth than a king in Hades.

In post-Homeric times, however, a surprising change occurred in the outlook on life. H. Romilly Fedden is mistaken when he writes in an otherwise scholarly study that "from Homer until the coming of the Stoics we get no idea of the burden of life."[7] Even the *Iliad* contains the observation "There is nothing more wretched than man of all things that breathe and are" (Book XXIV, 446 ff.). More specifically, the elegiac poet Theognis of Megara asserted in the sixth century B.C. that "it is better not to be born, next best to leave this world as quickly as possible." Sophocles writes in *Oedipus at Colonus,* "Not to be born is the most to be desired; but having seen the light, the next best is to go whence one came as soon as may be." Euripides, who also gives expression to this view, seems to be reflecting the Orphic conception of death as fulfilling the immortal soul's innermost desire to free itself from the prison of the body and rejoin its divine source. But no such interpretation was possible for Theognis who regarded death as total annihilation.

Whence arose this conviction that life is not worth living under any circumstances, not merely when it becomes unbearable because of severe illness, old age, loss of a loved one, or dishonor? Whether this was a widespread phenomenon or merely the opinion of some poets and a few disgruntled intellectuals is not really known. It is interesting that the historian Herodotus (fifth century B.C.) treats it as the correct view. After relating the story told by the Athenian statesman Solon (c. 639-c. 599 B.C.) of two youths from Argos who died in their sleep after they overexerted themselves in honoring their mother and thus had "a most enviable death," Herodotus adds that we have here "a heaven-sent proof of how much better it is to be dead than alive."[8]

Herodotus also provides us with some reasons for this view. His *Histories* are full of savage cruelty of men toward one another. One gets the idea of the barbarism and depravity of the times from the widely accepted rumor that the philosopher Democritus (c. 460-c. 370 B.C.), the father of "atomism," blinded himself because he could no longer endure witnessing the evils of his day.

Suicide in Retrospect

But this can be only part of the story. In any case, profound pessimism was not limited to the Greeks. Herodotus tells us that the Persian king Xerxes I (c. 519-465 B.C.), after reviewing his troops, suddenly burst into tears. Asked by his uncle Artabanus for an explanation, Xerxes replied: "I was thinking how pitifully short human life is—for all the thousands of men not one will be alive in a hundred years' time." "Yes," replied Artabanus, "but there are sadder things in life even than that. Short as it is, there is not a man in the world who is happy enough not to wish—not once but again and again—to be dead rather than alive. Troubles come, diseases afflict us, and this makes life, despite its brevity, seem all too long. . . ."[9] In India, toward the end of the sixth century B.C. the prince Siddartha Gautama, the future Buddha, decided to turn his back on the world when stepping out from his palace into the crowded streets he saw for the first time a sick man, an old man, and a dead man. From all these examples it would appear that between the seventh and fourth centuries B.C. pessimism and disenchantment with life were widespread and of an intensity never so far duplicated in human history. One is at a loss to account for it except by a massive "failure of nerve" afflicting the upper layers of society all over the ancient world. While the first part of Theognis's statement may be not more than an expression of pessimism springing from the disillusionment with the quality of life as it was at the time (and even with the "human condition" in general) the second part is clearly a call to suicide.

However, what effect this mood had on the incidence of suicide is not known. Any information is from a somewhat later period. For instance, toward the end of the Peloponnesian wars many Athenians expressed the wish that they were dead, but this was chiefly caused by their defeat. In any case, at that time there was an intensive search for a quick-acting and painless poison. According to the historian Xenophon (c. 430-c. 355 B.C.), hemlock was introduced in 403 B.C. There were other poisons, but Attic hemlock stood in the highest repute. Its efficacy can be judged by the description of its action on Socrates in Plato's *Phaedo*. But apparently it was not easily available, and there are reasons to believe that it was given to Socrates as a special favor, and the possibility of a quick and painless death may have been a factor in the refusal of the seventy-year-old Socrates to escape.

On the whole, however, the leading Greek philosophers, with the exception of the Stoics, were in principle opposed to suicide. Their views are discussed in detail in Chapter 13. Nevertheless in Alexandria under Ptolemy II (285-246 B.C.) suicide was publicly advocated; Hegesias, a philosopher of the Cyrenaic school, eloquently lectured on the miseries of life and his success was so great that, according to Cicero, "many among his listeners committed suicide."[10] Eventually Hegesias, who received the nickname of *Peisithanatos*—"the advocate of death"—was forbidden to lecture. However, there seems to have also existed in Alexandria (which during the two centuries B.C. was the world's cultural center, displacing Athens) during the reign of Cleopatra (69-30 B.C.) a school that taught suicide and the best means of achieving it, and some of the "students" were rumored to have committed suicide during sumptuous and extravagant feasts.

Cleopatra herself, one of the most famous suicides in history, used a rather unusual method—a snake bite—to put an end to her life. This was deliberate and symbolic, since according to an ancient Egyptian belief the snake was a minister of Amen-Ra, the sun god.

The Romans

Cleopatra's lover and political ally, the Roman statesman Mark Antony, committed suicide a few days before at receiving false news of Cleopatra's death. His was one of many

Roman suicides which occurred during the rule of Caesar Augustus. At the time there is said to have existed in Rome a sect which preached suicide. And according to the historian Valerius Maximus, contemporary of Tiberius (42 B.C. - A.D. 37), in the important port city of Marseilles the municipal senate supplied free poison containing hemlock to anyone who could give valid reasons for wanting to commit suicide.

In general, under the Roman empire suicide was not openly encouraged, and the government was officially opposed to it. But, as Helen Silving points out, "it is controversial whether suicide was generally punishable in Roman law."[11] There was, in any case, a permissive attitude toward it. The two main excuses were the miseries and afflictions of existence, and the feeling of boredom and of the purposelessness of life *("taedium vitae")*, but the maxim *Mori licet cui vivere non placet* (He is at liberty to die who does not wish to live) applied to both.

The numerous suicides among Christians during the time of Augustus and the following century were not due to such motives. Self-destruction was seen by them as a short-cut to a blissful afterlife. Also, they did not lay hands on themselves but let themselves be killed, often in a most atrocious manner.

In Rome suicide was punishable only when the interests of the state were involved, as with soldiers, or when property rights were affected, as when a slave killed himself. To escape legal punishment for a crime by committing suicide was also forbidden. While suicide committed "without cause" was punishable, suicide induced by "impatience of pain, or sickness, or grief" was exempt from punishment.

Interestingly enough, according to the historian Cornelius Tacitus (A.D. ?55-117) many committed suicide out of fear of execution, particularly since the property of those officially executed was confiscated, whereas those who killed themselves not only could safeguard their fortunes and pass them on to their kin but also received proper funerals. In the light

SUICIDE

of these facts, Nero's order to his teacher Seneca to commit suicide when he was suspected of having plotted against his former pupil appears as a kindness, especially considering the philosopher's enormous fortune.

In the Roman Republic, suicides of which records exist are predominantly of the heroic type. This is not surprising, since the distinctive characteristics of republican Rome were civic duty and moral virtue, and individual sacrifice for the common good was thoroughly consonant with these. Among the most famous were the deaths of P. Decius Mus in 337 B.C. in the battle near Vesuvius and that of his son Decius the Younger in 295 B.C. in the fight against the Gauls. The most glorified and admired was the suicide of Cato the Younger, Cato of Utica. Seneca declared of it that "Jupiter himself could not have seen seen anything more beautiful on earth." Cicero exalted it, and Horace devoted a poem to it. Cato, the great-grandson of Cato "the censor" who became famous because he ended all his speeches with the exhortation that Carthage must be destroyed, was a leader of the Republican party in the Senate. After Pompey's troops were defeated by Caesar, Cato transferred the rest of the army to Africa. Further reverses forced him to seek refuge in Utica but, realizing that he could not hold out there for long, he evacuated his troops. After the last transport left he decided to put an end to his life. His cause was lost and there was no reason to go on. Retiring to his quarters, he read passages from Plato's *Phaedo* and then stabbed himself. Pain made him lose consciousness, but when he revived he pushed away the physicians, tore off the bandages, and expired.

No less extraordinary was the case of Regulus, the consul who was a commander in the First Punic war (264-244 B.C.). He was captured by the Carthaginians and sent back to Rome to propose peace, giving his pledge to return whatever happened. Once in Rome, however, he argued strongly against peace and returned to Carthage knowing that certain death awaited him.

Another outstanding patriotic suicide was that of the

Suicide in Retrospect

Emperor Otho (A.D. 69) who, in order to terminate the civil war against Vitellus, chose to kill himself rather than to be the cause of further slaughter among his compatriots. Still another was that of the tribune Vulteius, a supporter of Julius Caesar. When his lonely ship accidentally stumbled on Pompey's fleet, he joined battle against impossible odds, and when finally overwhelmed committed suicide to avoid capture.

Suicide to avoid the ignominy of disease and the disability of old age is also a kind of "honorable" suicide, the idea being that man, the noble animal, ought not to allow himself to be reduced to doddering imbecility or subjected to a diseased body. Two such suicides admiringly reported by Pliny the Younger were those of his friends the statesman Corellius Rufus, and the poet Silius Italicus.

Fear of dishonor brought about the suicide of Cassius, the prime mover in the assassination of Julius Caesar. However, unlike Cato, he ordered his freedman to stab him.

Nero also had himself killed by an attendant. During his lifetime Nero had caused several suicides, among them those of his teacher Seneca, already mentioned, of Seneca's nephew, the poet Lucan, the author of *Pharsalia*, in A.D. 65, and of Petronius (A.D. c. 66), the probable author of the *Satyricon* and the most witty, elegant, and sophisticated Roman of his time. Since these were compulsory suicides in lieu of execution, there is a question whether they can be considered suicides if the intention to die is a decisive factor in the definition.

Memorable suicides among Romans were not limited to men. Perhaps the most impressive was that of Arria, the wife of the senator Caecina Paetus who was involved in a plot against the emperor Claudius. In order to give her husband courage she plunged a sword in her breast and then handed it to him with the words: *"Paete, non dolet"* (It does not hurt). One of the most celebrated suicides of antiquity, that of Lucretia, is said to have occurred much earlier, around 500 B.C. Lucretia, a married woman, had aroused the passion of Sextus Tarquinius. He threatened, if she did not yield to him, to kill her and to tell afterward that he did so because he found her with a lover. Next morning Lucretia told her father and her husband what had happened and then stabbed herself. This story has particularly impressed painters, including Tintoretto, Titian, Dürer, and Lucas Cranach, and dozens of lesser ones. These suicides, however, were relatively rare occurrences.

Suicide seems to have been popular for a long time in Rome's great adversary, Carthage. Its greatest general, Hannibal (247-183 B.C.) committed suicide when Rome demanded his extradition from his place of voluntary banishment. Before taking poison, which he habitually carried in a ring, the seventy-four-year-old hero remarked sarcastically that he wanted to deliver the Romans from the terror that an old man inspired in them.

As to the impact of pessimism on suicides in antiquity, there is no proof that it resulted in a notable increase in the number, but it was very probably conducive to the generally permissive attitude toward the act.

The Middle Ages

For the thousand years after the fall of the Roman empire, roughly A.D. 400 to 1400, there seem to have been few suicides. The permissiveness, even the encouragement, of suicide by the ancient Greeks was not immediately challenged by the new religion of Christianity. This is not surprising, since there is no prohibition or even criticism of suicide in either the Old Testament or the New. However, the promise of blissful immortality in the latter was a powerful incentive toward self-sacrifice for the early Christians. The overzealousness of the faithful in this respect, stimulated by the great veneration shown to martyrs, may have been a cause for the growing opposition of the early church fathers to suicide.

Suicide in Retrospect

By the end of the fourth century A.D. the categorical Christian rejection of suicide was vigorously expressed by St. Augustine (354-430). He considered suicide a crime and recognized no extenuating circumstances, even in the case of a woman who killed herself to avoid dishonor (or to expiate it, as did Lucretia). His main reasons are that suicide precludes the possibility of repentance, and that it violates the sixth commandment: Thou shalt not kill. Suicide is, in any case, a greater sin than any that one might wish to avoid committing by killing oneself. This intransigent position, which on the whole remains that of orthodox Catholicism to this day, presents certain difficulties, since some of those recognized as martyrs were suicides, and St. Augustine himself was forced to admit the possibility of exceptions. Thus he exonerates Samson by saying that he was acting under divine guidance and consequently exempt from the general rule.[12] Since Samson was not a Christian, one wonders why Augustine was so concerned about him.

St. Thomas Aquinas (1225-1274) enlarged on Augustine's view by condemning suicide because it is unnatural—that is, contrary to the charity which every man bears toward himself—and also because it is detrimental to the community and it usurps God's power to dispose at his discretion of man's life, death, and resurrection.[13] (Orthodox Protestantism is no less severe in its condemnation of suicide; perhaps it is even more uncompromising because it rejects the Catholic doctrine of purgatory, which provides a chance to expiate one's sins.)

The Church's prohibition appears to have been effective, and the psychological security provided by a unified and unchallenged world view which promised reward in the hereafter for all the inadequacies of this life undoubtedly worked as a suicide-inhibiting factor. On the other hand, during the Middle Ages, mass suicide was frequent among persecuted sects of Christian heretics and non-Christian minorities. Of the former the most striking example were the Albigenses in thirteenth-century France, adherents of the Catharic heresy, which substituted belief in a dualism—God versus Satan—for the Christian idea of God. In fact, the main tenets of the Albigensian doctrine indirectly favored suicide, for these included detachment from worldly concerns, rejection of private property, and avoidance of marriage insofar as it leads to the perpetuation of the human species. Their favorite method of suicide was the "endura"—a voluntary fast. The Russian "Raskolniki" (schismatics) of the early seventeenth century who clung to the "Old Faith" after the reform of the Russian Orthodox Church preferred the method of immolation, and several incidents of mass suicide in crowded churches and remote monasteries, especially when besieged by government troops, have been recorded.

The category of non-Christians included Moslems and Jews, who refused to be converted to Christianity and preferred to commit suicide. Characteristically, the method chosen by the latter was that used at Massada. Individuals did not kill themselves but were put to death by representatives chosen by lot for the task. There were also individual suicides among a class characteristic of those superstitious times—the witches. Suicides occurred also among wives of priests after celibacy of the priesthood was decreed in the eleventh century, and existing marriages of the clergy were broken up. There also seem to have been numerous suicides connected with epidemics, in particular during the time of the "Black Death," the plague which swept Europe in the fourteenth century, when people, terrified by the ever-present danger of imminent and horrible death, committed suicide.

The Renaissance

With the gradual emergence of the Renaissance spirit in the fourteenth and fifteenth centuries, a radical change in attitudes toward suicide occurred. What characterized the Renaissance was a new awareness of the world and its beauty and a feeling that life was wonderful. The somber *"memento mori"* of the late Middle Ages gave way to the new slogan proclaimed by the Florentine writer Francesco Guicciardini: *"Memento vivere!"* The combination of an unbounded *joie de vivre* and a new conception of man's relationship with God generated a faith in man's own forces and unlimited possibilities. Men became aware that, to a large extent, they were the masters of their own destiny. Pico della Mirandola (1463-1494) expressed this feeling in his famous *Oration on the Dignity of Man,* in which he has God say to man that he did not make him either a heavenly or an earthly creature, either mortal or immortal, but that "I created you so that as your own sculptor you make your own features. You can degenerate into an animal, but you can also be reborn through the free will of your own spirit into the image of God."[14]

But the shift toward appreciation of earthly existence and its pleasures enhanced the consciousness of life's transitoriness, which in turn led to a marked increase in the melancholy which that evokes. At the same time, the rediscovery of ancient writers and philosophers, which played such a decisive role in the formation of the new world outlook, reinstated death in its ancient function as an escape from the disappointments of life, which inevitably increased in proportion to the new great expectations. In the atmosphere of religious turmoil and growing independent thought, apologies for suicide began to appear.

In his *Praise of Folly* (1509) Erasmus, the great Dutch humanist, calls those who seek their own death in disgust at the nature of life "the next neighbors of wisdom."[15] His friend Sir Thomas More writes in *Utopia* (1516) that "whoever finds that his life is to him but a torment and dispatch himself out of that painful life acts wisely since by his death he will lose no commodity but end his pain."[16]

Not a few seem to have followed this advice, judging by the fact that in Shakespeare's eight tragedies there are no less than fourteen suicides. Among real-life suicides was the Italian scientist Gerolamo Cardano (1576). The most surprising among the apologists for suicide is the poet and divine John Donne (1572?-1631) who later became dean of St. Paul's in London. In *Biothanatos,* written in his youth and published by his son in 1644, Donne argues that the power and mercy of God are great enough to remit the sin of suicide, which the Church, following St. Augustine, considered a greater sin than any one might want to avoid by killing oneself.

Robert Burton in *The Anatomy of Melancholy* (1628) expresses a view similar to Donne's when he says about suicides: "What shall become of their souls, God alone can tell. His mercy may come ... betwixt the bridge and the brook, the knife and the throat." Burton shows considerable tolerance toward suicide: "What may happen to one, may happen to another. Who knows how he may be tempted?"[17]

The Eighteenth Century to the Present

The eighteenth century produced more clear-cut and forceful apologies for suicide. The most influential seems to have been that of Johann Robeck. Robeck's case is of particular interest since he wrote a major work advocating suicide and eventually killed himself. His posthumously published book[18] strongly influenced Jean-Jacques Rousseau. Although Robeck formed his views on suicide early, he turned his theory into practice rather late in life.

He was born on September 13, 1672, in Colmar (then belonging to Sweden) where his father was a prominent citizen, and became a brilliant student of the university at Uppsala. The study of ancient philosophy led him to accept the idea that the true philosopher is indifferent to life, even contemptuous of it. He concluded that if this view is taken seriously the logical conclusion is that one should prefer death to life and therefore, commit suicide. He argued that if the soul was mortal, suicide would do it little harm, since it would be annihilated whenever one's brief existence came to an end; if, however, it was immortal, suicide would render it a service by setting it free earlier.

Robeck planned to present a doctoral dissertation defending this thesis, but the rector of the university, who was also the archbishop of Uppsala, forbade him to do so. Robeck was offended, accused his fatherland of ingratitude and of not deserving to harbor a great thinker, and went into exile in 1704. He traveled all over Germany, was converted to Catholicism, and joined the Jesuits, for whom he undertook various missions. In 1727 he received permission to exercise clerical functions, to preach, and to hear confessions in a private estate near Hamburg. In 1734 he met a certain professor Funccius, to whom he wrote, a little more than a year later, that he decided to undertake, at the age of sixty-four, a last voyage. Because of melancholy which sapped his body as well as his spirit like a disease, he was going, like a sick man, to seek a change of air. His message concluded with the request: "Please publish the most important part of my manuscript and add to it a preface . . . ." In June 1735 Robeck departed for Bremen. From there he dispatched the rest of his possessions to Professor Funccius. Then he dressed with great care, got into a small boat he had purchased, and rowed out to sea. His body was washed ashore from the Weser River three miles from Bremen.

Robeck's suicide became famous. Voltaire refers to it in *Candide* (1759) where the old woman says that in her day she has seen an extraordinary number of people who hated their lives but only a bare dozen who have voluntarily put an end to them—"three Negroes, four Englishmen, four citizens of Geneva, and a German professor by the name of Robek."

The best-argued defense of suicide came from the great Scottish philospher David Hume (1711-1776) in his brief essay "On Suicide," which is discussed in detail in Chapter 13. An old argument was revived by Merian's *Mémoire sur le suicide* (1763), in which he held that suicide is neither a sin nor a crime but a disease. As did the rabbis of old, he saw suicidal people as to some degree mentally deranged, since otherwise they could not have gone against the natural instinct for self-preservation.

Obviously, the apologists and advocates of suicide did not remain unchallenged. In particular, Hume's permissive views were vigorously attacked in a book with the resounding title *A Full Inquiry into the Subject of Suicide* (1790) by Charles Moore. Moore's chief argument is religious, in that he sees suicide as interference with the design that divine Providence has for everyone. Even when "a man labors under the torture of an incurable disease, and seems to live only to be a burden to himself and his friends," he has "no excusable cause" for suicide. Although this was "thought to be a sufficient apology for the action in ancient days . . . in modern ones . . . it can be combatted by the force and energy of that true religion which both points out the duty and reward of implicit resignation."[19]

A similar position is taken by Madame de Staël in *Réflexions sur le suicide* (1813). Her main attack is directed against the view that suffering is an excuse for killing oneself: "It is not enough to hold with the Stoics that pain is not evil; one must convince oneself that it is a good," for it serves to "regenerate the soul."[20] Since God will never desert a true believer, one should never despair, Madame de Staël argues, and she also contends that suicide is not compatible with the dignity of man. An interesting feature of her views is that she, like Voltaire, considers financial ruin a main cause of suicide.

It is not without interest that in her youth Madame de Staël wrote a pamphlet in which she defended the right to suicide. Such changes of heart are not unusual but sometimes they go the other way. Napoleon, as a young general, declared in an Order of the Day that "a French soldier ought to show as much courage in facing the adversities and afflictions of life as he shows in facing the fire of a battery. Whoever commits suicide is a coward." Yet he himself made an unsuccessful suicide attempt on April 13, 1814, after his defeat at Waterloo.

The years from 1770 on were dominated by the Romantic Movement with its predilection for and even glorification of death. The poets Novalis and Jean Paul in Germany, Chateaubriand and Lamartine in France, Keats and Shelley in England, Lermontov in Russia found death infinitely desirable—as the return to the great All, as the golden gate to immortality, or simply as preferable to the ennui of living. To die by one's own hand became the "in" thing among young poets and literati, in words at least. But some did actually kill themselves.

Goethe's *The Sorrows of Young Werther* (1774) was inspired by the suicide of a young diplomat. Goethe himself could sympathize, even empathize, with his character, having gone through a similar turmoil *(Sturm und Drang)* himself. But *Werther* should not be taken as an approbation of suicide and even less as an apology for it. It is also a mistake to attribute to its influence a worldwide "epidemic" of suicides, for the simple reason that no such epidemic occurred.

In the nineteenth century the issue of the rightness or wrongness of suicide began to yield to the problem of its causes. Even the great literary works of that period, in which suicide occupied a prominent place (there are twenty-one suicides in the works of Balzac and thirteen in Dostoevski's five great novels), contain attempts to explain the phenomenon.

But the controversy over the morality of suicide is still going on. Among the most outspoken apologists of suicide is H. Romilly Fedden. He holds that

> more often than not the end of a suicide is a gain for the living. And in all those cases where suicide merely forestalls the process of disease and old age,

to speak of society's loss is beside the point. That suicide may be harmful to a certain section of society, the friends and relatives of the dead man, is sometimes true. As often as not, however, the suicide of the businessman saves his family, and that of the melancholy neurotic comes as a secret relief to those around him.[21]

The opposite view, based on religious considerations, is ably argued by the French philospher Léon Meynard. He maintains that "at bottom, all the reasons leading to suicide can be reduced to one—namely suffering. Disease, failure, misery, death are but some of the expressions, among many others, of the basic evil."[22] Consequently, the question of suicide inevitably involves a philosophy of suffering in the light of which it becomes possible either to condemn or to absolve suicide.

Meynard realizes that the problem which the fact of suffering raises in connection with the question of life's meaning is the larger problem of evil, "this stumbling block of all metaphysics and the great mystery of religion." The true reason for suicide is the refusal to submit to suffering. In order not to kill oneself one must know how to suffer. But to suffer in the name of what? Acceptance of suffering can be understood only in the religious perspective.[23] Meynard holds that "the existence of God is the supreme argument against the legitimacy of suicide."[24] The acceptance of suffering to the bitter end is justified by the fact that, for the Christian, to live is to carry a cross. Admittedly this is a paradoxical, irrational position, which the nineteenth-century Danish philosopher Søren Aabye Kierkegaard called the "scandal" of Christianity. To Meynard, however, the purpose of life is not happiness but purification through suffering. This view, which was held by the Christian saints, is no doubt a reversal of the natural inclination of man. But acceptance of suffering is not resignation—it is the use of suffering as a means of salvation.

Suicide in Retrospect

Religious philosophy does not justify evil; it makes two assumptions: that God exists and that He exists, not despite evil, but because of it. Evil testifies to the truth of God's existence and justifies human existence through the promise of immortality in a world freed from evil. What Meynard does not take into account, however, is the difficulty many people today have in accepting the religious answer.

2

FACTS AND FIGURES

According to official statistics, 21,281 people in the United States committed suicide in 1966; 21,325 in 1967; and 21,378 in 1968.[1] Probably many who read or hear these figures for the first time will be startled by the number of people who take their own lives. They may be even more shocked to learn that these figures, in spite of their apparent exactitude, are far too low—according to some experts, the actual number of suicides is perhaps one fourth to one third higher, or about 27,000 to 30,000 per year. The main reasons for this are that suicides are generally underreported because of religious and social considerations and that in many instances a coroner, even with the greatest professional skill and the best of intentions, cannot determine unequivocally whether a particular instance is an accident or a genuine suicide.

The stigma of suicide leads the victim's family to suggest, and sometimes the victim himself to simulate, a "natural" cause of death, and the widespread use and abuse of sleeping pills and other drugs contributes to the blurring of the real state of affairs. Some one-car accidents are in a similar category.

Facts and Figures

How does the estimated figure of 27,000 to 30,000 suicides per year in the United States compare to the incidence of suicide in other countries? Comparisons are made on the basis of the suicide rate per 100,000 inhabitants per year. However, several considerations must be borne in mind. The rate of 11.1 per hundred thousand for the United States is based on the official figures and not on the higher estimate. However, this rate does not reflect the difference in sex (16.5 for males and 5.1 for females), or the difference in color (whites 18, non-whites 9.6). In addition, there are regional differences. Thus in 1960 when the national rate was 10.6, the rate in Tampa–St. Petersburg, Florida, statistical area was 17.3, in San Francisco 17.2, and Los Angeles 17.1; these were the highest. But the Youngstown–Warren, Ohio, statistical area had the same rate as the national average, 10.6. Newark, New Jersey, with 6.9 and Providence, Rhode Island, with 6.7 were the lowest. There are also variations among countries in the efficiency of collecting the data as well as of determining the cause of death. For these and other reasons, a true comparison between countries is impossible.

Nevertheless, one can gain an approximate idea of how one's own country compares to others. Figures compiled by the World Health Organization on the basis of data supplied by the various member nations[2] show that among the lowest are Greece with a rate of 3.2 per 100,000 population; Northern Ireland with 4.8; Italy with 5.4; The Netherlands with 6.9; Norway with 7.7; and Canada with 8.8. Among the high rates are Switzerland with 18.4, Sweden with 18.9, and Denmark with 19.3, German Federal Republic with 20.0, Austria 22.8, Hungary 29.8, and West Berlin with 41.3. The United States has a lower-than-average rate, similar to that of England and Wales (10.8), Portugal (9.1), and Poland (9.0). Obviously, if the experts' estimate of the number of suicides is taken as the basis, the United States would be higher, closer to that of Japan (14.7) and France (15). But since in these as well as other countries suicides can safely be assumed also to be underreported, their rates would be correspondingly higher, so

SUICIDE

that the United States would remain in a median position.

In the light of this comparison it would seem an exaggeration to speak of the "tragedy of suicide in the United States." The incidence of suicide is much higher in many countries which otherwise compare favorably with the United States as far as social and political stability and physical and mental health are concerned. Interestingly enough, no comparison with the Soviet Union is possible. Although it is a member of the World Health Organization, it is the only country which does not furnish suicide statistics. Since it is otherwise very statistics-conscious, this is apparently in order to maintain the image of a perfect society.[3]

Nevertheless, the 27,000 to 30,000 desperately unhappy people who kill themselves in the United States each year are a lot by any standard; nationwide, this is about 80 persons a day. Worldwide, the daily figure has been estimated at more than 1,000. The real measure, however, of the problem of suicide—and of the extent of unhappiness in the world, if it is permissible to use this unscientific term as a common denominator for the multitude of motives for people's taking their own lives—is the number of those who try to kill themselves without attaining this goal (the "attempted" suicides). The number is estimated to be eight to ten times that of actual suicides, or four to five million people a year. And the number of people who seriously consider suicide as a "solution" to their difficulties but do not act on the idea is presumably several times the number of the "attempters."

In spite of their shortcomings, suicide statistics reveal certain facts, in particular about the differences according to sex, age groups, marital status (single, married, divorced, or widowed), and other information, which allow generalizations valid for most Western countries.

Thus, we know that suicide occurs much more often among men than it does in women. In 1964, for instance, the rate for men in the United States was three times that for women. While the suicide rate for both sexes that year was 11

Facts and Figures

per 100,000 population, the rate for males was 16.6 and females 5.8. On the other hand, many more women than men try to kill themselves and fail. As far as age is concerned, both sexes show a steady increase of the suicide rate with advancing age, except for the age group 65-74. Thus the suicide rate by age groups for both sexes per 100,000 population in 1964[4] was:

AGE:	5-14	15-24	25-34	35-44	45-54	55-64	65-74	75-84	85 and over
	0.2	6.0	11.9	15.6	20.5	22.7	22.1	23.9	25.3

The rates for non-whites are significantly lower than those for whites: all ages 4.6 compared to 11.6 for whites; 7.2 for males as against 17.2; and 2.2 for females as against 6.1. In the 15-24 age group the rate for both sexes is 4.9 compared to 6.1 in whites. But most recent studies among urban blacks indicate that the gap has been closing rapidly.

Some data are also available regarding the incidence of suicide among various professions. The most interesting finding is that the suicide rate among physicians is three times as high as that of the general population—36 per 100,000 as against 11—and that the suicide rate among psychiatrists has been calculated as twice that of physicians, approximately 70 per 100,000.[5]

3

METHODS OF SUICIDE

Although "death hath ten thousand several doors,"[1] means of committing suicide are relatively few. Some of them, like drowning, hanging, and jumping from high places are as old as suicide itself. Technological progress has not added many—firearms in the eighteenth century, domestic gas in the nineteenth, and "sleeping pills" in the twentieth. Frequency of use of a particular method today varies mainly according to country and sex. Thus "firearms and explosives" ranks first in the United States, but in Great Britain, where gun control is rigorously enforced, it ranks fifth. There domestic gas is in the forefront, with 437 males and 561 females out of 1,000 suicidal deaths by that means in 1959. In Germany hanging appears to be the most often used method, judging by the 1959 figures for Hamburg where 46 percent of males and 22 percent of females chose it, as against 1 percent for firearms for men and none for women. In France also, hanging was reported as the foremost manner of committing suicide in the 1950s, accounting for about 60 percent of the total. According to some, hanging was also the preferred method there in

Methods of Suicide

the mid-1800s, closely followed by drowning. But the information is contradictory. Thus between 1836 and 1846, among 1766 corpses in the Paris morgue 1414 were dead by drowning. However, Brierre de Boismont, who relied on court records, found that domestic gas occupied the first place, apparently because it was reputed to procure quick and painless death.

In the United States the "means of injury" and their percentage share for the year 1964 were as follows:

Sleeping pills and other pharmaceuticals	12.4
Other solid and liquid poisons	3.3
Domestic gas	0.4
Other gases	10.8
Hanging and strangulation	14.6
Drowning	2.6
Firearms and explosives	47.6
Cutting and piercing instruments	1.9
Jumping from high places	3.7

However, the use of some of these means fluctuates within short periods of time. In 1950 the first category, "pills," represented only 4.7 percent, and gas was 6.5 percent as against a mere 0.4 percent in 1964. Suicide by firearms, however, did not differ greatly, the 1950 figure being 43 percent.

As mentioned, the choice of means varies according to sex. Among women 30 percent used "pills," whereas only 6 percent of men chose this method. A higher percentage of women than of men chose drowning, though this, for centuries the favorite method of committing suicide among women, had shrunk by 1964 to an insignificant 2.6 percent of all suicides. Firearms were used by 56 percent of men and by 25 percent of women. It is surprising that so many women use this violent means of killing themselves, especially considering their greater abhorrence of disfigurement.

Some methods, such as immolation and voluntary starvation, are not included in the table, mainly because they are quite rare. The former, less uncommon in the Orient, possibly because of its similarity to widespread funeral practices, is the most spectacular way of committing suicide and therefore usually occurs in connection with some social or political issues to which the victim wants to call attention. Voluntary starvation may be more frequent than is generally assumed; it was frequently mentioned as a manner of committing suicide in ancient times.

If one uses H. J. Bochnik's distinction between "soft" and "hard" methods of suicide,[2] voluntary starvation is probably the "softest." This distinction is based, not on the degree of lethality, but on the seriousness of possible injury, in cases where the choice of method is influenced by a desire to preserve the integrity of the body. Perhaps a more fruitful distinction in elucidating possible connections between the choice of method and the personality of the suicide is that between "active" and "passive" methods. In the former, the suicide does something to himself; in the latter, he, as it were, lets something happen to him. In this perspective, shooting, stabbing, and even poisoning (although "soft") would be "active," whereas drowning and jumping from high places would be "passive"—the victim exerts only a minimum of effort but rather surrenders to the "elements." In suicide by drowning the concept of death as reabsorption into primal matter may be a factor. Neither of these distinctions, however, covers the variations within the categories. In the category of "firearms," there is surely a difference between shooting oneself in the temple, through the mouth, or in the heart region, as well as between using a pistol or choosing a shotgun which might completely destroy one's face. In Ernest Hemingway's case, was the choice of the shotgun significant, especially since he possessed the revolver by which his father killed himself?

The method used in a given suicide seems to depend on whether it is an impulsive act or a rationally planned and

Methods of Suicide

executed one, as when the victim carefully collects sleeping pills over a long period of time. There are also a number of bizarre suicides which show extreme ingenuity and careful planning and some of which are very difficult to fit into the usual categories. Thus, in 1833, a fifty-five-year-old Corsican, reportedly the son and assistant of the executioner of the city of Bastia, constructed a homemade guillotine and, by pulling a cord attached to the knife, cut off his own head. A similar case was reported to have occurred in 1847 involving a dealer at the Halles, the central food market of Paris.

In 1883 in Cattaro, Dalmatia (now Yugoslavia), a lieutenant of artillery killed himself by firing a cannon; standing at its mouth he lit the charge by means of a fuse attached to a stick. Soon afterward this method too was imitated, by a young French gunner. In the category "firearms and explosives" belongs also the suicide of a spectator at the theater in Cartagena, Spain, who killed himself on December 31, 1887, by placing a lighted stick of dynamite in his mouth. Instances of people blowing themselves up with hand grenades are not uncommon.

Some of the "tools" employed by suicidal people are quite ordinary objects, and the bizarre element derives from their use as a means to end one's life. Madame de Sévigné duly reported to her daughter on April 29, 1676, the manner in which the notorious Madame de Brinvilliers tried to kill herself: "... She thrust a stick, guess where? ... Not in the eye, neither in the mouth, nor in the ear ... but she would have been dead if help had not arrived promptly."[3] People try to kill themselves by swallowing, not only pills and all kinds of poisons, but combs, needles, nails, razor blades, keys, fountain pens, buttons, and crucifixes. Perhaps the most extraordinary suicide attempt was that of a Venetian shoemaker, Mathew Lovat, in 1810. Believing that he had received orders from "above" to die on a cross, he constructed one, crowned himself with thorns, and, covering his loins with white cloth, proceeded to crucify himself. He rested his feet on a plank affixed at the bottom of the cross and nailed them to it. Then he pierced his hands with 5-inch-long nails which fitted into holes previously drilled in the cross bar. Before fixing his left hand he made a cut in his left side. He then managed to push the cross to which he was attached through a window. There, since an elaborate arrangement of ropes was holding it in place, it remained hanging. He was observed and rescued the next morning and, before long, recovered from his physical wounds.

Bizarre methods of committing suicide, particularly because of the wide publicity they receive, are probably at least partly responsible for the still widespread view that all individuals who attempt or commit suicide are mentally deranged.

4

ATTEMPTED SUICIDE

One of the most interesting and significant facts about present-day suicide is that the number of people who try to kill themselves but survive is far greater than that of actual suicides. Although official statistics similar to those for suicides are not available, information about so-called suicidal attempts is obtainable from hospitals and private physicians. The two most competent studies using these sources—that of Shneidman and Farberow in Los Angeles, for the year 1957,[1] and that of Erwin Stengel in Sheffield, England, for 1960[2]— arrive at a ratio between attempted and completed suicides of 8:1 and 10:1 respectively. Both studies, however, emphasize that their estimates are probably on the low side. H. Jacobziner estimates that among adolescents the ratio may be as high as 100:1.[3]

What is the reason for this astonishing disproportion? Is it really so difficult to kill oneself? Or are the promptness and efficacy of medical intervention alone responsible for the high rate of survival? Certain characteristics of the survivors of suicide attempts, brought to light by the studies mentioned, may shed light on this problem. The number of women is far greater than that of men; the methods used are less lethal than those resulting in completed suicides; and the average age (between 20 and 30) is much lower than the median age of completed suicides, which is between 50 and 60. The incidence of mental illness is much less frequent—most attempters are merely "unstable personality types." Although manifest motives are on the whole the same as with completed suicides, ill health figures much less prominently than marital discord and unhappy love affairs.

Perhaps the most salient characteristic of many survivors of suicidal attempts is that they acted without premeditation, impulsively, out of rage, frustration, a sudden onset of despair or depressive mood. A fair number among them did not actually intend to die; others were satisfied to leave the decision to "fate." And those who merely wanted to blackmail the "significant other" sometimes even cooperate in their rescue by making sure that they will be seen while trying to injure themselves, or will be discovered in time to be saved.

These findings led Shneidman and Farberow to conclude that "it appears that one cannot combine attempted and committed suicides (and call them both suicidal) without masking ... differences, which can, in themselves, be extremely important."[4] Stengel is even more explicit, holding that attempted suicides and completed suicides ought to be considered as two distinct groups, or "populations," mainly in order "to call attention to obscured important aspects of suicidal attempts."[5] Stengel's distinction, however, has led to misunderstanding of his position. He does not think that there are actually two radically different "populations" and admits that his distinction is an "artificial" one aimed at correcting the "conventional approach to suicidal acts which is unduly restricted to those that are fatal." Where the distinction actually may be valid is with regard to the nonsuicidal ("normal") population as a whole.

Attempted Suicide

Important as it may be to be aware of the differences between attempted suicides and completed suicides, the conclusion that information gathered from the former is not applicable to the understanding of the psychodynamics of suicide is probably not warranted. More recent studies indicate that a much greater percentage than formerly assumed (as much as 25 percent) of those who attempted suicide subsequently did kill themselves and, interestingly enough, do not use more lethal methods than those used in their unsuccessful attempts. It has also been found that many more among the completed suicides than previously assumed had made earlier attempts. In addition, the prevalence of younger people among attempted suicides may relate to their more robust health, which enables them to survive injuries that would have been fatal to older people, while the prevalence of women may be partly attributable to their being biologically the stronger sex, a point made notably by the Swiss psychiatrist Pierre B. Schneider. Moreover, one should remember the fluid borderline between the two groups; even those who are merely "playing" at suicide may nevertheless actually kill themselves, and what was supposed to be not even a suicide "attempt" but a mere "suicidal gesture" may become a completed suicide. And sometimes people unequivocally determined on death may bungle the suicide or be prevented from killing themselves and thus become "attempted suicides."

Defining attempted suicide presents serious difficulties. Stengel, who rightly militates against the popular view of a suicide attempt as a mere bungled suicide, holds that even apparently harmless acts of self-damage ought to be considered as suicide attempts. He defines attempted suicide as "any non-fatal act of self-damage inflicted with self-destructive intention, however vague and ambiguous," and adds that sometimes this intention has to be inferred from the patient's behavior.[6] (The definition given by Shneidman and Farberow is "injuring oneself in a suicidal way with more or less lethal intention."[7]) Several points in Stengel's definition may be contested. As far as "self-damage" is concerned, there is none in the case of a person who steps out on the ledge of a high-rise building or climbs on the rail of a bridge with the intent to jump to his death. But this act is undoubtedly an attempted suicide, and, unless the individual can be talked out of his lethal design or caught in a net, it is almost certain to become a completed suicide. Regarding the inference of the real intent from the patient's behavior, while it may be prudent for the physician or psychiatrist to consider every self-damaged person as potentially suicidal, people nevertheless injure themselves when cleaning a weapon and drowsy insomniacs do forget that they have already taken a heavy dose of sleeping pills. A "pan-suicidal" bias on the part of the observer might make him see attempted suicide where there was none. Suicidal intent is very difficult to determine. Granted that suicidal acts are usually attempted or committed in a state of impaired judgment and that many suicidal people are ambivalent about wanting to die, if the apparent intention is markedly vague and ambiguous, the act should not qualify as attempted suicide. Otherwise, not only all "cries for help" but also all obviously manipulative self-injuries would fall into that category.

Perhaps the term of attempted suicide should be used only in the following situations:

1. When the suicidal act is bungled or fails because the efficacy of the method has been misjudged or its application was faulty
2. When the suicidal act is foiled—that is, when someone intervenes to prevent the act or its completion
3. When the possibly fatal outcome is frustrated by timely medical intervention.

Between these failed, foiled, and frustrated suicides and faked suicides are controversial instances which only thorough and unbiased investigation can correctly classify as attempted suicide, masochistic mutilation, or accident. The issue is the

Attempted Suicide

same as in cases where the cause of death is in doubt, except for the important advantage that the subject is still alive and can be questioned and studied. These instances mostly prove to be "cries for help," where the aim is not death but a change in conditions that are intolerable subjectively or even objectively. The amount of risk that the subject incurs in calling attention to his distress will indicate whether the act should be considered an attempted suicide. Other doubtful cases are injuries resulting from dangerous activities, because such activities are often assumed to be expressions of unconscious suicidal tendencies and sometimes even considered manifestations of these tendencies.

However, to see in the pursuit of all dangerous sports or dangerous occupations the workings of latent suicidal tendencies may be misleading. Many automobile racers, trapeze artists, and parachute jumpers, to mention only the most conspicuous examples, choose these occupations primarily for money, glory, and excitement; most of them look forward to retirement and old age, and not a few attain it. Risk-taking may well be a characteristic of all living, and this consideration makes labeling of injuries thus sustained as attempted suicide rather questionable. While many suicides gamble with their lives rather than unequivocally aiming at death, one must beware of generalizations and such false analogies as the comparison with Russian roulette. One wonders if the users of this analogy have ever seen a revolver or realize that in this "game" only one chamber out of five or six contains live ammunition, so that the chance of being killed or gravely wounded is 20 percent or even less. It is true that before the invention of the revolver, when firing mechanisms were not very reliable, some gambled on the chance that a loaded weapon would not fire. Such a situation is described in a famous story, "The Fatalist," by the Russian poet Mikhail Lermontov.

In instances where it is not certain whether the suicide attempt is genuine or merely simulated, the gravity of the injury (the degree to which it represents danger to life) is obviously not a sufficient criterion, and the seriousness or intensity of the desire for self-destruction must also be taken into account. Shneidman and Farberow distinguish between those who really want to die, those who leave survival to chance, and those who definitely expect to be saved.[8] The latter group ought not to be considered as attempting suicide at all. The term "pseudocide" was suggested by J. E. Lennard-Jones and R. Asher[9] for cases in which the patient is not in fact attempting suicide—that is, is not primarily oriented toward death. Neil Kessel later proposed the terms "deliberate self-poisoning" and "deliberate self-injury."[10] As the British psychiatrist Norman Kreitman has pointed out, these terms are unsatisfactory for several reasons. The patient may be deliberately poisoned but not suicidal, or suicidal and not poisoned in the toxicological sense. Moreover, omission of all reference to suicide "neglects the very real association that exists between 'attempted suicide' and 'completed suicide.' " He proposes instead the term "parasuicide."[11] In this connection, however, an even better term would be "protosuicide."

There is a definite need for a term that would distinguish between the cases of people who are not actually attempting to kill themselves and those of people who are. The term attempted suicide is not really satisfactory even for the latter, because every suicide in its initial phase is merely an "attempt"; it becomes a suicide only if death results. "Unsuccessful suicidal attempt" would seem more appropriate but this term is clumsy, and in addition students of suicide dislike any reference to "success" in connection with suicide. In any case it is doubtful that the term "attempted suicide" can be replaced, since it is deeply ingrained in everyday language and used by both authorities and mass media, even though it does not do justice to the wide variety of situations it is supposed to cover.

Whatever the inadequacies of the term, the fact that there are at least eight to ten times as many survivors as suicides reveals a remarkable situation. At any given moment, a considerable number of people are alive who at some time attempted suicide. Stengel estimates their number in the United States at two million. Ronald S. Mintz believes that there are at least five million.[12] An approximate figure can be reached by multiplying the annual number of suicides by ten; if this number is assumed to be 25,000 (somewhat higher than the official figure), the answer is 250,000. Since the average age of persons who have attempted suicide is between twenty and thirty and thus the individual has a life expectancy of another 30 to 35 years, the latter figure must then be multiplied by 30 (or 35), providing a total of between 6 million and 7 million persons. Because of the indiscriminate application of the label "attempted suicide" it is possible that the figure would include a great many cases that were not genuine suicidal attempts. However, it still represents a substantial reservoir, from which a sizable proportion of the yearly number of completed suicides is drawn. While it is disturbing to realize that so many people have felt at a certain moment of their existence that life was not worth living, it is reassuring to reflect that an overwhelming majority of these people will not again try to commit suicide; having received a second chance to choose between life and death, they have opted for the former.

The transformation of "genuine" suicides into "mere" attempters has become almost routine where special resuscitating facilities have been set up. With these, people who would have certainly been dead had they made their attempts a few years ago are now brought back to life. These instances may provide direct information on the psychodynamics of suicide, which was previously available only in cases where suicide notes were left. Among other things, such cases of "resurrection" may offer an opportunity to conduct a much-needed study of the reactions to having been saved among what one may assume to be hard-core unambivalent suicides and to determine how often these reactions are negative. In personal communications to the author specialists engaged in such rescue efforts have estimated the number of those who object to having been returned to life at a mere 2 percent. This corresponds to the conclusions of a study made in 1933 by W. Heimerzheim, who found that 70 percent of survivors called their suicide "stupid" or "silly" and only 2.2 percent were unhappy about having been saved.[13] These figures need verification, in particular since the subjects obviously represented a "mixed bag." For such a study to be valuable a method would have to be devised that would give special attention to the choice of interviewers and the timing of the interviews and provide other precautions to make it as foolproof as possible.

A Japanese study by K. Ohara, S. Aizawa, and S. Shimizu found that 90 percent were glad to have been saved, which means that 10 percent were not.[14] But E. C. Trautman, in a study of Puerto Rican immigrants, found that not a single one regretted having been rescued.[15]

5

SUICIDE AMONG ADOLESCENTS

Suicide among young people shocks and disturbs us more than any other kind of death, because it cannot be blamed on "nature" or "fate" and because it takes place at a period of life which is supposed to be the happiest, when the vital force is at its peak and when one has "the whole life before him." The concern over juvenile suicide dates back to the last quarter of the nineteenth century and the beginning of the twentieth, when reports of frequent suicides among high-school and university students came to the attention of the authorities and the public in several European countries and in Russia. This concern is reflected in particular in Dostoevski's *Diary of a Writer* for the year 1876. It was also the reason for the special symposium of the Vienna Psychoanalytic Society in 1910, which is discussed in Chapter 6. The alarm was justified, since a survey of nineteenth-century statistics undertaken in England early in this century by A. MacDonald showed considerable and sometimes extraordinary increases.[1] The First World War put an end to this concern, as well as to the upward trend in juvenile suicides; instead the cream of European youth was sacrificed on the battlefields.

When the interest in juvenile suicides revived several decades later, after the Second World War, D. Mulcock in England made a signal discovery. He divided the available data into two groups, ages 8 to 14 and 14 to 17, and found that a "sudden and dramatic spurt" in the incidence of suicide takes place with the onset of puberty. He also found that during the Second World War suicides increased among English boys, while the rate for girls remained constant. These figures were in marked contrast to the decrease in suicides among the adult population in the same period.[2]

What is the suicide rate among young people in the United States, and how does it compare to that of other countries? In the period 1951-53, for the age group 10 to 14 the rates were very low—0.7 per 100,000 populations for boys and 0.2 for girls—as compared to West Germany with rates of 1.9 per 100,000 for boys and 0.5 for girls. But in England and Wales the rates were even lower than in the United States—0.2 for boys and 0.1 for girls. For the same period in the age group 15 to 19 the United States rates were 3.9 for males and 1.6 for females. These compare rather favorably with Japan: 26.1 and 18.7 respectively; Switzerland: 16.9 and 6.4; and West Germany: 12.1 and 6.8. The lowest rates were those of Norway, 2.0 for males and 1.0 for females.[3]

Since that time there has been a marked increase in the suicide rate among the young in many countries. In the United States, for the age group 15 to 24, the figures for 1962-63 showed increases over those for 1952-53 of 35 percent for white males (82 percent for nonwhites) and 45 percent for white females (81 percent for nonwhites). The rates per 100,000 for 1962-63 for the age group 15 to 24 were: white males 9.3, nonwhite males 8.0, white females 3.2, nonwhite females 2.9.[4]

It is noteworthy, however, that the suicide rate in 1964

was lower than that of 1934. The United States rates for the last four decades[5] were:

	ages 15-19	ages 20-24
1934	4.6	10.8
1944	2.8	6.0
1954	2.4	6.0
1964	4.0	8.4

Thus suicide rates among the young were rising in 1964 compared to the very low rate of 1954 and falling compared to the much higher one of 1934. Nevertheless, a trend toward rising suicide rates since 1964 has been confirmed by the most recent statistics compiled by investigators of the Los Angeles Suicide Prevention Center.[6] According to that study, the rise among people in the 20-to-29 age group has been dramatic. The rate in 1969 was 28.4 per 100,000, which is even higher than the rates among people between 55 and 75 (22.7) and for people over 75 (23.9). Surprisingly, the study also showed that the rate for nonstudents was higher than that for college students, which until recently was the highest in that age group.

Juvenile suicides are particularly puzzling because the young have, as the saying goes, "everything to live for," and youth, at least in retrospect, appears as the best part of one's life. The question arises whether suicides of the young ought not to be considered as being in some respects different from those of adults. The factors suggested as playing a role in juvenile suicides are as varied and as numerous as those in suicides of adults, and on the whole of the same nature, but there is a difference in emphasis and some conditions are specific for the younger group. Thus fear of punishment, shame over failure, and anxiety and guilt over sexual matters may be stronger than in adults and such fear and shame involve school and college instead of profession or social position.

SUICIDE

Almost universally, children, especially when they have been punished, unjustly as they feel, have the fantasy, "If I die, my parents will be sorry." On the other hand, the suicide of a parent may prompt its imitation by a child. In such cases a partial motive may be a desire for reunion with the dead parent, complicated by the fact that the child does not realize the finality of death. Some investigators have found that spite and revenge are the most frequent reasons for suicide or suicide attempts in young children.

For older age groups suicide is less frequent among married than among single people, but among the young the opposite is true. There is no evidence that either books (serious or inferior) or the newspaper publicity given to suicides have any noticeable influence on juvenile suicide. Drugs, in particular LSD, seem to act primarily as catalysts for underlying conflicts and suicidal predispositions, although, as Sidney Cohen, an authority on LSD, has pointed out, the use of LSD may be related to suicide in several ways.

André Haim, the author of the only full-length book on juvenile suicide published to date, advances the interesting idea that perhaps the real causes of suicide among the young should be sought in their being adolescents. In particular, he asks whether adolescence as such does not embody the desire for death and a natural tendency to seek it. Is it not possible that at the moment when human beings become capable of starting their own lives they have a tendency to refuse to do so? The adolescent is particularly prone to overstep the boundary between a thought and its execution; he is given to acting out; he questions himself and the world, and is often acutely preoccupied with death in general, his own death, and suicide. He has to adjust to his changing body and a new, powerful sexual drive and often feels great uneasiness in relation to both.[7]

However, Haim rejects the temptation to consider adolescence the cause of juvenile suicide, because numerically very few juveniles kill themselves and because clinical facts do not bear out this hypothesis.⁸ However, he calls attention to some specific traits which appear regularly in juvenile suicides, in particular a mood which cannot be designated as depression but is rather moroseness and permanent dissatisfaction, an unrealistic and megalomanic ego-ideal, lack of critical acumen and the demand for "absolutes," general "impatience," and inadequate defense mechanisms.

Haim emphasizes our ignorance of the psychodynamics of juvenile suicide, except for a few correlating factors: a "broken home," lack of integration into a peer group, death of the father during adolescence, failure in school, and so forth. The vital question of the origin of suicidal tendency remains open. Haim thinks that it is necessary to start almost from scratch: verify what is assumed to be known, clarify definitions, and improve statistics; he concludes that, in fact, his book "terminates with questions without answers."⁹

6

THE SEARCH FOR CAUSES

Earlier in this book I have often had occasion to refer to reasons, or, to use a psychological term, motives, for suicide. The main source of knowledge about what produces suicidal behavior is provided by suicides themselves, who, in verbal communications to members of their family, friends, or neighbors prior to the act, in suicide notes left behind, or in statements made after a failed or frustrated suicide attempt, indicate the reason, or reasons, that drove them to the step.

The most frequently cited among these, according to several studies, are ill health and the pain connected with it, unhappy love affairs, loneliness, and marital strife. Less frequent are financial difficulties, humiliation, remorse, revenge, and a host of other motives usually grouped in studies under the label "miscellaneous." Which among the motives more often mentioned is the leading one varies according to the surveys which reflect cultural background, age, sex, and occupation of the suicidal population under investigation. Sometimes ill health, sometimes unhappy love appears at the head of the list.

The Search for Causes

In any event, it is interesting and instructive to look at concrete examples of the explanations of the suicidal act given in suicide notes, or "last messages," left by the victims.

Ill health combined with financial difficulties was cited as the reason for the suicide of Friedrich List (1789-1846). List, an outstanding political scientist and economist, was put in prison because of his democratic ideas. He later emigrated to the United States and then returned to Germany as a United States consul. Illness and his political past made it impossible for him to provide for his family, and he killed himself. His last letter to a friend follows.

> My dear Kolb, I have started to write at least ten times to my admirable wife and to my children but I couldn't bring it off ... my headaches and distress grow stronger every day, in addition, the horrible weather ... and then the future—without income from my writings I would have to use up my wife's "capital" (since I have none) and which is not even enough to take care of her and the children. I'm close to despair. God have pity on my family. Whatever you and other friends will do for them, God will reward you.

Perhaps the best-known and the most romantic double suicide in recent history was that of the Archduke Rudolf (1859-1889), heir to the Austro-Hungarian throne, and the eighteen-year-old Baroness Mary Vetsera. The latter left the following letter:

> Mayerling, January 29, 1889.
> My dear sister, we are both going blissfully into the uncertain Beyond. Please think of me once in a while and marry only for love! I couldn't do that and, since I couldn't resist love, I'm going with him.

SUICIDE

The message from the thirty-year-old archduke is addressed to a friend, Duke Miguel of Branganza, and reads:

> Dear friend, I must die. I could not have acted differently. Keep well. So long, your Rudolf.

The loss of a loved one is the principal reason given by Jean-Marie Roland (1734-1793), a prominent Girondist and the husband of Marion Roland, who also played a prominent role during the French Revolution and was guillotined by the Jacobins. The following note was found on his body after he stabbed himself:

> Whoever you may be who has found me, do honor to my death. My whole life served only the purpose of being useful. I died the way I lived: virtuously and honestly. I didn't leave my hiding place out of fear but because of indignation when I found out that my wife was murdered. I didn't want to remain any longer on an earth which was defiled by innocent blood.

The sensational suicide of Uriel Acosta (1590-1647), a contemporary of the philosopher Baruch Spinoza, was brought on by humiliation. Acosta was a descendant of "Marranos"—literally "pigs," Spanish Jews who nominally converted to Christianity because otherwise they would have faced death, or at best exile. At the age of twenty-two he began to doubt the truth of Christianity. He went to Amsterdam where he was converted to Judaism, but soon thereafter he came in conflict with the rabbis and was expelled from the Jewish community. After several years, he was readmitted but under conditions so humiliating that he refused to accept them and shot himself. The following is an excerpt from his testament, *"Exemplar humanae vitae"*:

The Search for Causes

No word and no gesture of contempt is strong enough for my adversaries who maintain they have decreed this exemplary punishment over me in order that no one would ever again dare to oppose their will. ... I have more right to find you guilty for all that you have done to me, the way you have degraded me until my life has become loathsome to me.... A free man must know how to live or at least, how to die honorably.

Disgrace and resentment motivated the suicide of a noted Austrian biologist, Paul Kammerer (1880-1926). He wanted to prove that acquired characteristics are transmitted, faked the evidence, and was exposed.

Letter to whosoever finds it:

Dr. Paul Kammerer begs not to be brought home so that his family should be spared the spectacle. It would be the simplest and cheapest way to use the body in a dissecting laboratory of a university. This would be also most agreeable to me since, in this way, I would render a small service to science. Perhaps my esteemed colleagues will find in my brain a trace of what they missed in the living expressions of my intellectual activity. Whatever happens to the corpse—burial, cremation or dissection—its owner didn't belong to any denomination and wishes to be spared any kind of religious ceremonies which would probably be refused to him anyhow. This is no animosity against individual priests who are as much persons as all the rest and often are very good and noble persons indeed.[1]

The following case is of particular interest because its acknowledged motive was despair over the meaninglessness of human life in the godless universe of modern science. Julius Haiduk, an Austrian school teacher, wrote to the principal of the high school at which he taught:

> I beg of you, esteemed Herr Director, to receive kindly this, my last letter, even though it is written by a suicide, and to be charitable in judging this, my last act. I have expended all my energies to acquire broad knowledge and education. But, as a result, my feelings have become impoverished and all enjoyment of life has died in me. The endless routine of soulless teaching could not fill the emptiness in me. We form skillful technicians and argumentative pseudo-intellectuals but do not educate man for true joy and divine virtue for which he was created. The new science which I have studied with such application has emptied the heavens of God, has de-spiritualized the world, and has degraded it to a mere soulless interaction of cogs in a dead mechanism. Such an existence is not worth living. Filled with disgust, I am withdrawing from it. Forgive me if by this auto-separation I am bringing sorrow to you and to my friends and wish me from the bottom of your heart the eternal rest I have eagerly desired for so long. Yours, J.H.[2]

In considering these cases one is immediately struck by the fact that there might have been solutions other than suicide. List's situation can be compared with that of Jean-Jacques Rousseau who spent his whole life in ill health and abject poverty, solved his financial problems either by sponging on generous friends or doing hack work such as copying musical scores, and "took care" of his five children by placing them in foundling homes. Spinoza had greater troubles with his co-religionists than Acosta but did not let these interfere with his work or studies. As to the suicide of Archduke

The Search for Causes

Rudolf and Mary Vetsera, about half a century later King Edward VIII of England abdicated his throne in order to marry the woman of his choice. True, there were great differences between these two cases. Rudolf had a wife; his father, the Emperor Franz Joseph, was a prude and very strict, and since both Rudolf and Mary Vetsera were Catholics, divorce was out of the question. By the same token, however, suicide was a mortal sin, which they were willing to take upon themselves.

The point is not moral condemnation of the suicides described, or the possible argument that, for instance, List's act was more noble than Rousseau's behavior, but the fact that the reasons given by the suicides obviously do not tell the whole story, since the overwhelming majority of people in similar situations do not commit suicide. The question then is why these particular people did kill themselves.

The scientific study of suicide, which was pioneered in the first half of the nineteenth century primarily by the French psychiatrists Jean E. D. Esquirol and A. F. Brierre de Boismont, has produced an impressive body of literature, and has become particularly active since 1955, seeks to discover the real motives or causes of suicidal behavior. Although there are still wide-ranging disagreements and considerable confusion in terminology, there are important points of agreement. The disagreement is mostly a matter of emphasis—that is, whether interpersonal relationships, intrapersonal conflicts, or biochemical aspects are being stressed—and this depends on whether suicide is being studied by sociologists, psychiatrists and psychologists, or biochemists. The terminological confusion is mostly but not exclusively due to semantic laxity. Such terms as causes, motives, factors, determinants are often used interchangeably. On the other hand, terms such as contributing causative factors, precipitating factors, conscious motives, secondary causes, unconscious motives, principal causative factors, principal causes, and so forth, are all indications of the difficulty of establishing the real motives as well as the causes of suicide. More importantly, they indicate the prevailing view that no single motive or cause can adequately account for suicide and that many diverse psychic forces and social circumstances predispose a person toward and precipitate the suicidal act.

It is not easy to determine the respective shares of the psychological and sociological factors in any particular instance of suicide, or even in attempted suicide where the psyche and circumstances of the subject are available for scrutiny. One such factor is loneliness, which many consider to be the common denominator of most suicides and which Walter Pöldinger demonstrated to be a deeper motive in suicides arising from unhappy love affairs, marital discord, and sickness.[3] Sometimes social factors—widowhood, divorce, unemployment, imprisonment—are the principal causes of loneliness, but the psychological makeup of the individual also may prevent him from establishing normal social relationships when these are possible. Whatever its roots, loneliness is certainly an important precipitating factor or motive of suicide. (Actually, the term "precipitating factor" is more correctly applied, not to a complex like "marital discord," but to a single act, such as one partner's leaving the house after a violent argument.) However, the role of interpersonal conflicts and the suffering that people inflict upon one another should also not be underestimated. Thus, when Pöldinger finds confirmation of Paul Valery's dictum, "Suicide is the absence of the others," it would be well to remember Jean-Paul Sartre's statement, "Hell is the others."

Both loneliness and interpersonal conflicts are motives for suicide, rather than causes, a distinction which Robert Gaupp insisted upon at the beginning of the twentieth century.[4] For Gaupp the causes of suicide are the biopsychical driving forces, which often do not even rise to the consciousness of the individual and thus cannot constitute motives, but which are related to race, age, sex, work, and social status. This valuable distinction has been narrowed down among the psychiatric profession to refer only to abnormal mental states.

Thus Pöldinger defines as the cause of suicide "those psychopathological states within which suicidal thoughts and impulses arise and are carried out,"[5] as does another leading student of suicide, Erwin Ringel, who sees suicide as "the conclusion of a pathological psychic development."[6] This widely accepted view is not as radical as Esquirol's position, since the psychopathology here means neurotic rather than psychotic disturbances. Esquirol wrote:

> All that I have said up to now, the facts which I have reported, proves that suicide presents all the characteristics of insanity [*alienations mentales*] of which it is but a symptom; that there is no point in looking for a unique source of suicide, since one observes it in the most contradictory circumstances, and because it is symptomatic or secondary, be it in acute delirium, or chronic; besides, the autopsy of suicides made so far did not throw much light on the subject of pathological changes.[7]

Accordingly, "the treatment of suicide belongs to the therapy of mental illness ... and one has to have recourse to treatment proper to each kind of insanity in order to treat an individual who is propelled toward his own destruction."[8]

However, Brierre de Boismont, the author of the first great modern work on suicide, written two decades after Esquirol's work and including more than 5,400 cases, takes a much less restrictive view. In his concluding remarks, Brierre de Boismont states that

> ... the examination of causes ... proves that a sharp difference separates the suicides of reasonable people from those of the insane. The motives invoked by the former are, in effect, taken from the passions, desires, regrets—in short, all the ordinary

motivations of life. With the latter, on the contrary, the suicidal tendency is determined by hallucinations, illusions, delirious conceptions, a morbid irresistibility, a true pathological state, which the symptomatology of suicide of the insane establishes in a most evident way. Finally, freedom is preserved by the former, while it does not exist or is heavily restricted in the latter.[9]

Thus explicitly recognizing the existence of suicides of "reasonable" people, Brierre de Boismont attributes them to the "impairment of moral character" which makes it impossible for them to withstand what he calls "reverses of fortune," whatever these may be. It must be mentioned in this connection that Esquirol may not have been completely blind to the possibility of suicide by "normal" people, since he stressed the importance of religious beliefs and moral precepts and noted that a person lacking them "will be more disposed than others voluntarily to end his existence as soon as he experiences some unhappiness or some reverses, for he will be disarmed against the sufferings of life."[10] Eighty years later, H. W. Gruhle, in his monograph on suicide, did not add anything new to Brierre de Boismont's dictum when he described nonpsychotic suicide as "the failure of the personality before a situation."[11]

In order to follow the historical sequence of the attempts to understand the causes of suicide it is necessary to leave psychiatry for the time being and look in another direction. While Esquirol was formulating his views on suicide, Auguste Comte (1798-1857), a former instructor at the Ecole Polytechnique in Paris, subsequently secretary to the French social philosopher, Count de Saint-Simon, was evolving a new science to which he gave the name of sociology. Not having been able to obtain a position at a university, Comte gave lectures about his ideas to a private audience which included some prominent thinkers of his time. These lectures were published as *Cours de philosophie positive* in six volumes between 1830 and 1842. Interestingly enough, Esquirol was among the auditors, which may explain why he stressed the fact that social and environmental conditions are likely to disturb an individual's emotional equilibrium.

Comte himself mentioned suicide only once, and in a rather unexpected connection. An outspoken adversary of supernatural religion, bent on replacing Catholicism with his own "religion of humanity," he nevertheless praised the Church for its uncompromising condemnation of suicide, since such an attitude has great social value. "The more afterlife loses its moral efficacy, the more important it is that all individuals should be attached to present life."[12]

Comte's view of suicide as an "antisocial practice" was shared by Emile Durkheim, who inherited from him the task of making sociology a true science. Durkheim's *Le Suicide* marks a new departure in the attempts to understand suicide. The necessity to combat suicide, since it runs counter to the last remaining collective sentiment—the ideal of humanity—was probably as much responsible for Durkheim's turning his attention to the subject as was the circumstance that available statistical data on suicide appeared to him to be the perfect basis from which to infer the laws of social life. In the process he provided a sociopsychological theory of suicide.

Durkheim's fundamental idea was "collective representations," which in a given society constitutes a "collective consciousness." These representations are "collective" rather than "universal" and exist outside of the individual consciousness, on which they operate "coercively." They can be determined directly, not through the medium of the thoughts and emotions of the individuals, but by examining their permanent expressions in written law, works of art, literature, and, most important, statistical averages. Suicide statistics insofar as they represent suicide rates and not the circumstances attending individual suicides, are then a "social fact." But Durkheim did not always adhere to this purely sociological approach.

His other basic concept was that of "social solidarity"; this was the key to distinguishing social types and to the distinction between "normal" and "pathological," with which the practical application of sociology becomes possible. The normal is relative only to a given social type at a particular time, but it merges with the average, which yields "an objective criterion," allowing us to distinguish between social health and social disease. "Healthy," as Charles Darwin implied, is that which is advantageous to society, and the sociologist, like the physician, should try to "maintain a normal state."

Applied to suicide, the sociological approach of Durkheim means that although suicide appears to be a personal act, it can be explained only as resulting from the state of the society to which the individual belongs. The suicide rate expresses the suicidal inclination of a society. Should the character of the society change, so would its suicide rate. If there is much "anomie"—that is, abnormality—in a society's structure, there will be more suicides. But a certain number of suicides are inevitable. The number is determined by the extent of individual integration with the social group—the family, the professional organization, the religious community.

The degree of integration is the basis for Durkheim's classification of suicides as egoistic, altruistic, or anomic. Egoistic suicide results from lack of involvement with the society and concern with it. Exaggerated individualism leads to a weakening of the control which society exercises over the individual and exposes him to the collective suicidal inclination. The opposite is the case with altruistic suicide, in which excessive concern over the community and an exaggerated sense of duty lead to self-destruction. Most suicides related by Greek and Roman historians, as noted earlier, belong to this type. The Japanese hara-kiri and Indian suttee also fall into this category, neither being really voluntary but rather the result of social pressure, as do instances of old and sick people who kill themselves in order to cease being a burden to their families. Although the number of altruistic suicides in the modern Western world is relatively small, they usually receive great publicity and their perpetrators are admired and respected. Anomic suicides are caused by disturbances and disorganization in the social organism, the pathological social situation which Durkheim called "anomie." As a result of this situation, society's influence on the individual is lacking and thus his immunity against suicidal inclination is weakened. When religious beliefs decline and codes of conduct are relaxed or disregarded, suicides increase. The supposed higher frequency of suicides in non-Catholic countries and the high rate among divorced and unemployed people are examples of anomic suicides.

Most suicides obviously belong to the first type, the egoistic, simply because they do not fit into either the altruistic or the anomic category. The distinction between anomic and egoistic suicide is often impossible to draw. It is difficult to determine when a state of anomie prevails, and moreover suicides motivated by sickness, mental illness, financial ruin, and unhappy love affairs—that is, those most frequently occurring—may be linked with a lack of integration with society but very rarely with the state of "anomie."

Jack D. Douglas points out that Durkheim was concerned almost exclusively with the latter two types of suicide but "distinguished them from each other only inconsistently, and generally in terms of individual rather than social causes."[13] Douglas's scholarly work contains a valuable presentation of the historical context of Durkheim's theory, a thorough analysis of *Le Suicide,* and a detailed critical account of post-Durkheimian sociological theories of suicide but suffers from the same defect that Douglas finds in Durkheim's book: it is "extremely difficult and very confusing."

Even though Durkheim's basic contention that "society" or "social reality" (however defined) is the fundamental cause of suicide has not gained wide acceptance, his monumental work, as well as subsequent studies inspired by it, have called attention to the suicide-producing factors in society—social isolation, unemployment, retirement, old age, and social maladjustment.

When, some thirty years after the appearance of *Le Suicide*, the French sociologist Maurice Halbwachs undertook the task of bringing up to date the work of his teacher Durkheim, he stated that "in closing this work, more than one reader, especially more than one philosopher, has without doubt had the feeling that the problem of suicide does not present itself any more and that, henceforth, its solution was known."[14] It would be more correct to say that most had the contrary feeling—that as far as suicide is concerned the answer to the riddle must rather be sought in the "heart" and mind of man. In fact, Halbwachs himself later came to the conclusion that social and psychological explanations are not mutually exclusive but complementary.

Meanwhile the depth-psychology of Sigmund Freud claimed to have found the key. Psychoanalysts first came to grips with the problem of suicide in 1910, when a small group which at the time constituted the Vienna Psychoanalytic Society met with Freud and a well-known educator, David E. Oppenheim, to discuss what looked like an "epidemic" of suicide among high-school pupils. Alfred Adler, who presided at the meeting, presented a view of suicide based on the theory expounded in his book *Organic Inferiority and Its Psychical Compensation* (1907). Suicide, like neurosis, is a "childish form of reaction to a childish overestimation of motivations, humiliations and disappointments. It represents, like neurosis and psychosis, an escape by anti-social means from the injustices of life." Isidor Sadger stated that "nobody commits suicide who has not given up hope for love." These were not exactly original views. Even Wilhelm Stekel's more provocative statement that "no one kills himself who did not want to kill another or, at least, wish death to another" can scarcely be seen as a momentous contribution if one considers that there is probably no person who has not at some time wished death to another, yet relatively few commit suicide. Still, adumbrated in this statement was an idea which became important in later psychoanalytic explanations of suicide. As for Freud, he merely pointed out that no light has been shed on the main problem—namely, how it becomes possible for the powerful instinct of self-preservation to be overcome.[15]

When, a few years later, Freud ventured an explanation, he suggested that the psychic energy needed for self-destruction originated in the wish to kill someone else and that the intended victim was someone whom the suicide had loved and identified himself with in the past; because this person could not or ought not to be killed, he could be destroyed only if the suicide in whom the other "lived" killed himself. In other words, aggression is actually directed against the "internalized" other, and in this interpretation suicide appears, as Shneidman graphically puts it, as "murder in the 180th degree." One may speculate to what extent the German word for suicide, *Selbstmord*—that is, self-murder—may have influenced this view, but, as Litman points out, Freud's is a rather complicated explanation involving a host of psychoanalytical concepts like introjection, identification, ego-splitting and regression.[16]

It would have been surprising if Freud had remained satisfied with this explanation. He was troubled also by other issues—in particular, the relation of aggressive instincts to the basic sexual instinct. As he himself described it later:

> After long hesitancies and vascillations we have decided to assume the existence of only two basic instincts, Eros and the *destructive instinct*. The aim of the first of these basic instincts is to establish even greater unities and to preserve them, thus, in short, to bind together; the aim of the second is, on the contrary, to undo connections and to destroy things. In the case of the destructive instinct, we may suppose that its final aim is to lead what is

living into an inorganic state. For this reason we call it the *death instinct*.... In biological functions the two basic instincts operate against each other, or combine with each other. Thus the act of eating is a destruction of the object with the final aim of incorporating it, and the sexual act is an act of aggression with the purpose of the most intimate union. This concurrent and mutually opposing action of the two basic instincts gives rise to the whole variegation of the phenomena of life.[17]

The concept of the death instinct (actually Freud used the term *"Todestrieb"*—death drive—and "instinct" is a mistranslation) was first put forward in 1920 in an essay entitled "Beyond the Pleasure Principle." The main purpose of the death-drive theory was to explain the phenomenon of masochism, but it also provided an explanation of suicide. If there is indeed in everyone, alongside the instinct of self-preservation, such a powerful push toward death, suicide would be simply a breakthrough of the "death instinct" induced by some pathological condition. Indeed some psychoanalysts considered it precisely that. An often overlooked consequence of the assumption that we all instinctively seek our own destruction is that it makes aggression toward others appear as a deflection of our more basic hostility toward ourselves. Thus, using Shneidman's expression, murder can be said to be suicide in the 180th degree!

The foremost American exponent of the death-drive theory, Karl Menninger, distinguishes three components in the suicidal act: the wish to kill, the wish to be killed (since "one who nourishes murderous wishes also feels, at least unconsciously, a need for punishment of a corresponding sort"[18]), and the wish to die. All three are usually unconscious and it is interesting that Menninger does not consider the *conscious* wish for death as an undisguised expression of the death instinct. "The death instinct is probably much more evident in the activities of daredevils than in the pessimistic musings of the melancholy patients and philosophers." [19] These three deeper motives of suicide "are complicated by extraneous factors—social attitudes, familial patterns, community customs, and also by those distortions of reality incident to an incomplete personality development." But neither these alone, nor heredity, suggestion, or maladjustments, can explain suicide, which is due to self-destructive tendencies "first appearing long before the consummation of the critical act." [20] The latter point is of importance in understanding Menninger's concepts of "chronical" and "partial" suicides. He considers as such all behavior resulting in self-injury—for example, alcohol addiction, drug abuse, asceticism, martyrdom, risk-taking activities, and "purposeful" accidents. All are expressions of the "death instinct."

The trouble with the explanation of suicide by means of this instinct is that its existence is more than problematic. [21] (Even the majority of psychoanalysts no longer accept this hypothesis.) From the point of view of the search for the true cause of suicide, it is a pity that there is not better proof for a self-destructive tendency in man as postulated by Freud than some instances of suicide in which a ruthless drive toward self-annihilation is clearly evident. This is too narrow a base to uphold the theory of the two basic instincts, and, beyond that, of a vision of the world in which "the two immortal adversaries—Eros and Thanatos"— are locked in a ceaseless and apparently endless struggle.

But even if the existence of the death instinct had been proved, the question of why it manifests itself with such force only in a few cases would remain. This question is as crucial as Freud's original one—how is it possible for the powerful instinct of self-preservation to be overcome? Had Freud found an answer to that question, he would not have needed to postulate the death instinct. Now it is necessary to ask how the death instinct breaks through or is released. If there is indeed such an instinct, one may speculate that what "releases" it in a particular instance may well be the same force that overcomes the instinct of self-preservation, or to put it differently, a factor or factors by which the equilibrium of the two basic drives is disturbed. One of the possibilities obviously is mental disorder in the individual, which corresponds to the view not only widespread among the general public but shared by students of suicide, that only persons who are mentally ill kill themselves. Such a view, if justified, would dispense with the necessity of looking for other causes of suicideal behavior. It has also other "advantages," such as providing an excuse for suicidal acts and exonerating them from the religious and moral points of view, easing the conscience of the "significant other" whom the suicide may blame for his act, shifting the burden from social factors, and making suicide prevention a strictly psychiatric issue.

The validity of this view is examined later. First, however, it is necessary to mention the explanation of suicidal behavior derived from the "goal-reflex" theory of the Russian psychophysiologist Ivan Pavlov (1849-1936). In a paper written in 1916 Pavlov declares that "all of life is the fulfillment of a single aim, namely the preservation of life; it is the unceasing activity of what is commonly called the life instinct." In a man this instinct takes the form of the goal-reflex, which, Pavlov says,

> is the basic form of life-energy in every one of us. Life is full and strong only in those who strive all their life toward some goal even though not always completely attainable, or go enthusiastically from one goal to another.... Life ceases to be attractive as soon as the goal disappears. Do we not read quite often in the notes left by suicides that they terminate their life because it has no purpose or goal?... The tragedy of suicide consists precisely in that in most instances merely a momentary impediment, or as we physiologists say, a "blocking" of

the goal-reflex occurs, and only in rare cases is this impediment a lasting one.[22]

Thus the high incidence of suicide among adolescents is explained by their inability to envision broad goals and perspectives which makes it hard for them to cope with difficulties, and which is due to lack of experience or faulty education. The impediment of the goal-reflex explains also the suicide among older people and those afflicted with an incurable disease. This explanation, which implicitly admits the possibility of suicide among mentally normal people, does not affect, even for those who accept it, the recognition that the majority of suicides are suffering from mental disorders.

7

SUICIDE AND MENTAL DISORDERS

A frequently encountered opinion, already mentioned, holds that since killing oneself, for whatever reason, is "against nature" no "normal" person would commit such an act. This view has been countered by the argument that many suicides are deliberate and carefully planned and thus could not be the product of an "unbalanced" mind. However, those who contend that no sane person would kill himself point out that only mentally ill persons could behave so singlemindedly and "rationally" in a matter involving such a grave issue as life and death. Another argument against the uncompromising insanity theory of suicide refers to instances where suicide is not only socially acceptable but even prescribed in certain circumstances. This argument is met by the objection that these suicides are entirely different from those usually occurring in daily life and encountered in psychiatric practice.

It is clear, however, that the suicidal act should not be regarded as the sole criterion of mental disorder and that the only way to resolve the controversy is by investigating the possible presence of mental illness prior to the act. Unfortunately, several studies bearing on this problem, made in recent years in various countries, have yielded results which vary on the frequency of mental disorders in persons who have committed suicide from as low as 20 percent to as high as 94 percent.[1] The principal reason suggested for these discrepancies is that investigators differ in their concepts of what constitutes mental disorder, some limiting it to psychoses, psychoneuroses, and "clinical" depression and others taking a broader view to include neuroses and "psychopathic" reactions to stressful situations. Another explanation is the frequent absence of reliable information about the mental health or illness of the suicides when no medical psychiatric records are available. Information based on interviews with persons close to the suicide is open to criticism on several counts. Where the information indicates mental disorder, the question of competence in evaluating abnormal behavior by laymen arises. When it does not, the lay opinion that the suicide behaved normally prior to the act may be caused by a desire to avoid blame for not having sought professional help. To add to the difficulties, there is no way of determining, let alone measuring, the state of mind of a suicidal individual immediately preceding the commission of the act.

The situation is different in cases of attempted suicide. Interestingly enough, four of eleven studies containing information about mental disorders among attempted suicides indicate its presence in all the cases under investigation (that is 100 percent), and none shows an incidence of less than 74 percent.[2] These findings are the more puzzling since it is being generally held that psychotics are more prone to completed suicides, and neurotics to attempts, and the latter are not usually considered as suffering from mental disorders in the strict sense of the term. Be this as it may, the question of the incidence of mental disorders, however defined, among suicides leads to the question of what kind of disorders are most responsible for suicide. In a study of psychiatric patients in a Veterans Administration hospital Alex D. Pokorny arrived at the following suicide rates per 100,000 per year: organic, 78; neurosis, 119; personality disorder, 130; alcoholism, 133; schizophrenia, 167; depression, 566.[3] These figures are particularly interesting, not only because they indicate the proportion of the different disorders but also because they clearly show the preponderance of depressive illness (of which different types are being distinguished) in bringing on suicidal acts. Suicidal thoughts and impulses appear practically in every depression. There is, however, considerable disagreement among students of suicide with regard to the extent to which depression is responsible for suicide, the results of studies varying between roughly 25 and 75 percent. This is quite different from the question of the rate of suicide among the depressed. The figure most often cited is 5 percent, or 500 times the national suicide rate of 0.01 percent (11 suicides per 100,000). But some consider even this figure too low. F. N. Pitts, Jr., and F. Winokur give a figure of 16 percent among patients with manic-depressive disorders and also cite several studies made since 1938 in different countries in which the percentage is found to be between 13.4 and 15.3.[4]

In other words, as far as the incidence of depression among suicidal persons, and the rate of suicides among the depressed are concerned, it would seem to be not far wrong to say that while possibly as many as half of actual suicides are afflicted by some form of depression, "only" 5 to 15 percent of the depressed eventually commit suicide. Both figures, however, convey the particular and grave problems which depression presents to the psychiatrist called upon to deal with it as well as the therapist engaged in suicide prevention. To the former, suicide is the constant and dreaded possibility, the only occasion when he comes professionally in contact with death. To the latter, unless he happens to be a physician, the presence of "clinical" depression in the suicidal patient gives a feeling of helplessness and impotence, since he realizes that, in such cases, his psychotherapeutic "tools" alone are of no avail. For both, the difficulties are aggravated by the fact that suicidal wishes increase with the severity of depression, regardless of whether it is "endogenous," that is, one assumed to be caused by a biological derangement in the organism, or "reactive," brought on by an upsetting event such as loss of job, bereavement, or financial reverses.

The types of depression just mentioned are not meant to prejudge the continuing debate about the definition and classification of depressions.[5] Here it is sufficient to note that, despite theoretical controversies, significant progress in treating various kinds of depressions has been made in recent years, which have seen, in addition to psychotherapy, the emergence of electroconvulsive therapy (ECT) as well as significant advances in pharmacotherapy. With regard to the latter, it has been found that special care must be exercised in the selection of appropriate antidepressants, because of the frequent and often dangerous side effects. As far as suicide is concerned, some antidepressants intensify the anxiety and distress of the patient, and thus increase his suicidal tendency; there is also the danger that all antidepressant drugs may be used by the patient as a means of killing himself.[6]

The fact that depressed patients show a high percentage of spontaneous recovery[7] is one bright spot in an otherwise dark picture. However, the ever-present danger of suicide reappears if depression recurs, as it is generally greatest at the onset of the depression and soon after the patient has been discharged.

In the light of what has been said about the prevalence of depression among suicidal people, and considering the complexity of suicidal motivation, the controversy over whether suicide is an act of courage or cowardice becomes to a large extent meaningless. Those who, following Aristotle, claim that the suicide is a coward justify this position by saying that he is obviously afraid of life. Those who praise his courage think of their own and most other people's fear of death, which the suicide apparently is able to overcome. These explanations are both gross simplifications. Fear of death is by no means absent in suicidal persons. Moreover, such simplistic views overlook the variety of notions of death entertained by different people. To some death may not mean total annihilation, but blissful afterlife, rebirth, or reunion with dead loved ones, an idea which has prompted not a few suicides. Both views of death—as the end or as leading to an afterlife—may be suicide-promoting or suicide-inhibiting, depending on individual circumstances, but as a rule they do not play a decisive role. More often than not, the subjects did not give much thought to death *per se* but rather did not want to live any more. Perhaps the statement "I want to die" has to be clearly distinguished from the statements "I don't want to live any more" or "I had enough" as indicating differences in suicidal motivation as well as in the mentality of the suicidal individual. It may be a mistake to speak of the wish to die when the wish may actually be to escape the ordeal of living. For the purposes of suicide prevention, however, it may be useful to discuss the notions of death held by a potential suicide in order to neutralize their possible suicide-promoting potential.[8]

As far as cowardice with regard to life is concerned, it is more a question of the individual's threshold of resistance to stress, pain, and worry, his ability to cope with crisis (Charles Zwingmann's "Krisentoleranz,"[9]) than of anything else. Sir Thomas Browne's standard—"when life is more terrible than death, it is the truest valor to live"—is not only too high for most but totally unrealistic as far as passing judgment upon suicidal individuals is concerned.[10]

8

SUICIDE PREVENTION

The idea that something could and should be done to prevent suicide was put into effect only in the twentieth century. The first counseling service for suicidal people in the United States, and probably in the world, the National Save-a-Life League, was founded in New York in 1906. Paradoxically, this happened at a time when the burning issue was the right to suicide, which was beginning to be tacitly recognized by the majority of educated opinion. Legal sanctions against suicide had either been abolished or had ceased to be enforced in most civilized countries, although the act was still socially taboo. Moreover, the prevailing view of suicide among professionals was unfavorable to the establishment of such a service. Suicidal people were regarded either as insane and therefore belonging in an institution or as doomed to suicide by heredity and therefore beyond salvation. Clergymen, however, frequently came in contact with desperate people who talked about committing suicide. Naturally they tried to talk them out of the idea and in many instances found that this could be done. Thus it was no accident that a Baptist minister, Harry Warren, was the founder of the National Save-a-Life League.

The movement initiated by Warren did not spread, and it was nearly fifty years later, in 1953, that the Reverend Chad Varah founded in London the Samaritans, an organization not unlike Alcoholics Anonymous. This movement emphasizes the social and religious arguments against suicide, referring to physicians only those people who are obviously mentally ill. The main technique consists in "befriending"—that is, giving friendship, care, and love to people in despair. The Samaritans have succeeded in establishing branches throughout Great Britain and the British Commonwealth.

In the meantime, the view on suicide among the professionals had also changed. Important monographs reflecting the new approach were published by psychiatrists Gregory Zilboorg (1936) and Karl Menninger (1937) in the United States, by Gruhle (1940) in Germany, and by Deshaies (1947) in France, and Durkheim's *Le Suicide* was translated into English (1957).

The real breakthrough in suicide prevention came in 1958 when the Los Angeles Suicide Prevention Center was established with the help of federal funds. It was founded by the psychologists Edwin S. Shneidman and Norman L. Farberow, who, together with the chief psychiatrist of the Center, Robert E. Litman, made it a model for this type of facility. The center maintains a 24-hour telephone service, functions as a short-term clinic, and carries on research into suicidal phenomena. Gradually centers were set up in various other cities, and as a result of encouragement by the Center for the Study of Suicide Prevention, established in 1966 by the National Institute of Mental Health, about 200 prevention centers throughout the United States are now functioning actively.

Similar centers were also established in Europe at about the same time as in Los Angeles, the best known being those in Vienna (founded by Erwin Ringel) and in West Berlin (founded by Klaus Thomas). Important research on suicide, in particular in its relation to depression, is carried out at the Psychiatric Clinic of the University at Basel, Switzerland, directed by Professor Paul Kielholz and his assistant Walter Pöldinger. The latter's table for assessing suicidal risk is reproduced in the Appendix of this book.

As a result, much new knowledge about suicidal behavior has been acquired and many misconceptions have been dispelled.[1] There is now general agreement that not all people who try to kill themselves are mentally ill, that most suicidal "crises" are of relatively short duration, and that much suicidal behavior is a cry for help. The assumptions that people who talk about suicide never kill themselves, and that suicidal people are fully intent on dying have been found to be false. Other false assumptions are that suicide is prevalent either among the very rich or the very poor: suicide is "democratic"; and that suicide is hereditary: suicide does not "run in the family" and the belief that it does only increases the suicidal risk.

But there are also widespread misconceptions about the activity of suicide prevention centers. People often protest that those who, because they are tired of life or for other valid reasons, want to do away with themselves should not be prevented from doing so. Such people do not realize that there is no conflict between suicide prevention and the position that suicide is an inherent right of each individual. In the first place, prevention is not compulsory. At the same time, why should not those who cry for help be able to get it? Suicide prevention does not need any justifications beyond those cited by its proponents: the ambivalence of most suicidal persons, the passing nature of suicidal crises, and the serious psychological trauma that suicide causes in the survivors. A further argument, however, is that many suicidal people have gifts and talents which can benefit society.

An entirely different kind of objection to suicide prevention is raised by the Jungian psychotherapist, James Hillman, in his book *Suicide and the Soul*.[2] There the concept of suicide prevention is criticized on the ground that death is merely an "experience," that the "soul" (although Hillman himself "defines" this as "a deliberately ambiguous concept resisting all definition") may need the death experience in order to undergo a radical change, and that "for some souls organic death through actual suicide may be the only mode through which death experience is possible." Hillman's main argument is that "we do not know if the soul dies." He also asks, "If the soul insists on organic death through suicide, cannot this too be considered an unavoidable necessity, a summons from God?" But only if Hillman's various and questionable assumptions are accepted can his position regarding suicide prevention be justified.

A much more realistic problem in connection with suicide prevention is its effectiveness. Actually, this comprises two problems. One is the overall effect of the activity of suicide prevention centers on lowering the suicide rate of a nation, the ideal target being its reduction to zero. The other is the evaluation of the effectiveness of a given center.

In a recent British study, Christopher Bagley tried to evaluate the effect of the Samaritans on the suicide rate by "an ecological method"—that is, by comparing the changes in suicide rates of towns where the Samaritans operate with an equal number of "control" towns, which are generally similar, "given present knowledge of urban characteristics," but in which Samaritans do not as yet operate. He found that in Halifax the pre-Samaritan rate was 17.7 per 100,000; five years after the Samaritans became active the rate dropped to 12.97. In the "control" town of Leeds, in the same period, the previous rate of 11 per 100,000 rose to 13.2. Bagley concludes that "the evidence points to the possibility, although it by no means offers proof, that Samaritan schemes may directly lower suicide rates."[3]

No such statement can be made in connection with the

center in Los Angeles, where the rate has not been reduced and according to some has actually increased. Two explanations have been advanced to account for this phenomenon. The first is that, precisely because of the activity of the center, suicide statistics have become more realistic. In particular, the center's close cooperation with the coroner's office and the use of the "psychological autopsy" initiated by the center have caused a number of apparently accidental deaths to be correctly recorded as suicides. The second explanation cites the self-imposed restraint in publicizing the center's existence, which was due partly to the small size of its staff and the financial limitations preventing expansion and partly to the concept that the center is primarily a research and training facility, so that its activity was too restricted to have affected the suicide rate. In a follow-up study of patients for the year 1962 Litman points out that "in Los Angeles where there are approximately 1200 suicides a year, one would need to prevent about 300 suicides in order to establish an obvious and significant decrease in the suicide rate. For this the center would have to contact 35,000 suicidal patients a year.[4] But in the first ten years of the center's existence only 26,000 people were in contact with it.

As to the effectiveness of the center in preventing suicides, a survey of patients for 1967 by Dr. Carl Wold, its chief psychologist, estimates that about 1 percent went on to commit suicide.[5] Assuming that such an estimate is applicable also to the other years (even though Litman's survey for 1962 gave an estimate of 4 percent), this would mean that among those who contacted the center over the ten-year period about 260 persons ultimately killed themselves. The question is how many of those 26,000 would have committed suicide if they had not contacted the center.

A way of arriving at a rough estimate could be based on the ratio between completed suicides (s), attempted suicides (a), and what one could call "suicide contemplators" (c). The assumption is that all those who contact the center are at least "contemplators." (Litman's distinction between acutely suicidal and chronically suicidal persons is not taken into consideration, since he assumes that suicide is distributed evenly between the two categories.)

The ratio between attempted and completed suicides is recognized by most authorities to be between 8:1 and 10:1. The ratio between contemplators and attempters is an empirical figure that differs for every center and from year to year. A sample of 984 cases of general suicide prevention center population studied by Wold shows that 52 percent had a prior suicide attempt, and 31 percent a recent attempt. If the latter figure is used, the ratio between contemplator and attempter *(c:a)* for this group is roughly 3:1. Thus, if the ratio between attempters and suicides *(a:s)* is assumed to be 10:1 and that between contemplators and attempters 3:1, the ratio between contemplators and suicides is *(c:s)* 30:1. The *probable* number of suicides among the contemplators in the absence of suicide prevention center intervention can be expressed as

$$c/(c:a) \times (a:s).$$

According to this formula, 26,000:30 would have committed suicide had they not had contact with the center, or roughly 860 persons instead of the 260 estimated by Wold to have done so. In short, it can be assumed that the Los Angeles center has prevented at least 600 deaths in the ten years of its operation.

It is obvious, however, that no matter how efficient and well distributed suicide prevention centers may be there are definite limits to their effectiveness inherent in the complexity of suicidal behavior. Thus there will always be a certain number of impulsive suicides, as well as of people so firmly set in their suicidal resolve that they would not even consider availing themselves of prevention facilities. There is also an even more basic reason which is simply that prevention ought to begin much earlier than the onset of the suicidal crisis. An obvious example is the "broken home," which according to numerous studies figures prominently in the life histories of suicidal people. The lack of unanimity in defining "broken home" (most often used to designate the loss or absence of at least one parent for a prolonged period) is in itself indicative of the variety of adverse conditions that may arise within the family unit. If unfavorable events in childhood are added to the unavoidable vicissitudes of adult life in society, nothing short of the elimination of the sociogenic factors in suicide—"a revolutionary change in social living" (Stengel)[6]—could provide a genuinely effective prevention.

9

THE PSYCHOLOGICAL AUTOPSY

The inexactness of suicide statistics has already been pointed out. Not only countries but counties and cities of the same country differ in the efficiency of determining the cause of death. The competence of coroners and medical examiners varies considerably, and when suicide is in question, pressures may be exerted toward concealing it, because of the stigma attached. Last but not least, there are frequently genuine difficulties in determining whether a suicide has in fact taken place, particularly when no suicide note is left, which is the case in 80 to 85 percent of all suicides.

There are other considerations besides statistical exactitude which make an unequivocal verdict of suicide a matter of great importance. Criminologists may face the problem of murder disguised as suicide; insurance companies are interested in being able to apply the clause in life insurance policies which excludes coverage in case of suicide; and while survivors may want to hush up the suicide of a family member, it often happens, particularly in our pill-addicted society,

The Psychological Autopsy

that suspicion of suicide will remain attached to what was in effect an accidental overdose and cause a trauma in the minds of the survivors. In short, there are also legal, economic, and psychological reasons for devising a better method of determining suicidal deaths.

One such method, supplementing the medical post mortem and routine police investigation, is the "psychological autopsy" developed by Shneidman and his colleagues at the Los Angeles Suicide Prevention Center. By interviewing families, friends, and acquaintances of the deceased the Death Investigation Team of the center endeavors to reconstruct the victim's life circumstances, medical history, state of mind preceding his demise, previous suicide attempts if any, addictions to alcohol and drugs, and so on. This consulting team is called in by the medical examiner-coroner of Los Angeles County whenever a case is provisionally classified as "Accident-Suicide Undetermined."

To give an idea of the kind of cases these are, the body of a twenty-three-year-old single woman, apparently beaten unconscious about the head, was found in a garage. Police investigation disclosed that she was a prostitute, a chronic alcoholic, and a drug addict and had been involved in a fight during an "orgy." Homicide, however, was ruled out, and the preliminary verdict was acute barbiturate intoxication. But the psychological autopsy found two previous suicide attempts. On the basis of this and other facts, the certification of Probable Suicide was issued.

Another case concerns a fifty-year-old woman found dead in her bed. The case was reported as natural death resulting from acute drug intoxication. The psychological autopsy revealed an appalling array of tragic events in the life of the victim. She had seen her first husband burn to death; her mother had died in an explosion during an operation; her father was a sadistic alcoholic; she had had several nervous breakdowns and had made one previous suicide attempt. Intolerable pain from a severe back injury had made her a drug addict in an effort to find relief and caused her to say on several occasions that she could not bear her suffering much longer. As a result of these findings the team recommended certification of the mode of death as Probable Suicide.[1]

Dr. Theodore C. Curphey, former chief medical examiner of Los Angeles County, considers the psychological autopsy very useful and effective. In an interview in 1969 he pointed out that of 188 drug deaths in 1953, before psychological autopsy was used, 74 percent were certified as suicides, 11 percent as accidents, and 15 percent as undetermined. In 1962, after the introduction of psychological autopsy, these percentages were significantly altered: of 440 drug deaths that year, 90 percent were certified as suicides, only 1 percent as accident, and 9 percent as undetermined. Drug deaths—now extremely frequent in California—are sometimes very difficult to certify without the aid of the psychological autopsy. The actress Marilyn Monroe, for example, was taking three different kinds of drugs and could have died accidentally. But the psychological autopsy revealed not only her suicidal state of mind prior to her death but also the fact that she had made several attempts at suicide previously.[2]

Much less frequent are instances in which all indications seem to point to suicide but in fact either murder disguised as suicide, or a freak accident, has taken place. One of the most interesting cases of this kind occurred in France, in August 1830, at the chateau of the old and enormously wealthy Prince Condé, duke of Bourbon. A valet discovered the duke's body propped against a window, his right cheek leaning against an inside shutter, as if listening to some noise outside. The duke's private physician ascertained that his patient was dead but also discovered that he was hanging by his neck, the noose consisting of two handkerchiefs tied together. A peculiar detail was that the victim's toes touched the floor. Everything pointed to suicide. The duke was not only old but in poor health. He was also known to have been despondent because he had a young mistress, the Baroness de Feuchères, of whom he was extremely fond, and was unable to demonstrate his affection in the way that he was accustomed to.

There was, however, one circumstance which seemed to rule out the possibility of suicide. Because of an old fracture the duke had no use of his left arm, and on his right hand, as the result of a wound sustained in battle, three fingers were missing. Yet the knot of the noose was so complex that it clearly required a dexterity of which he was incapable. Was it, then, murder? Robbery was quickly ruled out since the duke's jewel box was found untouched in its usual place. There might have been other motives for murder, and there were rumors to that effect, especially since the baroness had formerly been a prostitute. But no conclusive evidence was ever brought forward. Thus accident remained the other alternative, a quite unlikely possibility except for a bizarre account given by the baroness.

According to her, she was fond of the duke and eager to help him achieve his heart's desire. Like most of her contemporaries, she was an avid spectator at public executions and consequently aware that when a man is strung up by the neck, an erection occurs. She decided to utilize this knowledge in order to restore to the duke the capacity of making love. She claimed that her lover found the method effective and the experience rewarding. On several occasions he let himself be "hanged," and the baroness untied the noose in the nick of time. But on the fatal night she was unfortunately not quick enough—whether deliberately or subconsciously will never be known.

Interestingly enough, although her story was accepted as true, the official verdict was suicide, on orders of King Louis Philippe. The original investigating magistrate, who insisted that suicide was out of the question, was dismissed by the king. The monarch had good reasons for his action. One of his sons, the Count of Chambord, was the heir to the duke's fortune which was estimated at over 120 million francs. The slightest hint of murder would have led to a protracted investigation and freezing of funds. On the other hand, the accident version given by the baroness was not only scandalous but suspect. However, she seems to have taken an active part in persuading the duke to name the count as his heir, a little service for which she not only deserved to remain unmolested but to receive, as was rumored, a 10-percent commission.

An earlier case of a similar nature was that of the composer Franz Koszwara, which, however, took place not in a ducal palace but in a prostitute's flat. A native of Prague, Koszwara settled in London in the 1780s and his composition "Battle of Prague" (1790) had an extraordinary popular success for the next several decades. But poor Koszwara did not enjoy his fame for long. On September 2 of the same year, he visited Susannah Hill, a lady of easy virtue. After having consumed considerable amounts of brandy, he asked her to hang him for five minutes, since this would help to maintain his ardor. Susannah went out and bought a rope and performed the duties of a hangman. When she cut Koszwara down, he fell to the floor unconscious. A physician was called but could only ascertain that the composer was dead. Miss Hill was accused of murder but was acquitted. Musical histories listed Koszwara as a suicide under mysterious circumstances until the facts came to light.

Recent scientific literature describes several cases of such "hangings" aimed at stimulating the male genitals and achieving orgasm; when these result in death they may be mistaken for suicide.[3] But such instances are relatively rare. Most cases in which an unequivocal determination of suicide may be difficult are concerned with drugs—overdoses of sleeping pills, unawareness of the lethality of simultaneous intake of tranquilizers and alcohol, or overdoses of dangerous drugs by addicts.

10

TERMS AND DEFINITIONS

The word "suicide" is of relatively recent origin. Although it is eventually derived from the Latin, it was never used by the ancient Romans. Instead, they employed circumlocution: *"sibi morten consciscere"*—"to procure one's own death"; *"vim sibi inferre"*—"to cause violence to oneself"; *sua manu cadere*"—"to fall by one's own hand." The word "suicide" first appears in English about the middle of the seventeenth century. Edward Phillips (1630-?1696), in his philological dictionary, *New World of Words,* claims to have invented it: "One barbarous word I shall produce, which is suicide, which I had rather should be derived from 'sus,' a sow, than from the pronoun 'sui' ... [since] it is a swinish part for a man to kill himself."[1] Until then the word used was "self-murder."

The German equivalent for "self-murder," *Selbstmord,* came into general use much later, in the late eighteenth and early nineteenth century. Until then, the word was *Selbsttötung*—self killing. The German philosopher Immanuel Kant uses this term, as well as *willkürliche Entleibung,* which means discretionary act of killing oneself. As to *Selbstmord,* he points out that one can use it only if it is assumed that the act is a crime.[2] In addition to *Selbstmord* and *Selbstmörder* (one who commits suicide), there is in German another popular term for the person who commits suicide, namely *Lebensmüder*—one tired of life, which clearly contradicts the aggressive implications of "murdering oneself" and stresses helplessness and hopelessness. There is also another word for suicide, *Freitod,* freely chosen death, with the connotation that suicide is the highest expression of man's freedom. Probably as a reaction to the implications of these terms one finds in German scientific literature on suicide more and more frequently the term *Suizid* (which is meaningless unless one knows the English or French word "suicide"). Another frequent term is *Selbstvernichtung,* which means self-destruction, a term now used increasingly in the United States.

In France the word *suicide* had made its appearance by the middle of the eighteenth century. A supplement to the Jesuit journal *Mémoires de Trevous,* published in 1752, attributes its introduction to Abbé Desfontaines (1737), who defined it as murder of oneself. The French philosopher Montesquieu (1699-1755) referred to *homicide de soi-même* or *mort volontaire*—voluntary death, though Voltaire in his 1778 commentary on Montesquieu's *De l'Esprit des lois* used the word "suicide," which, in the same year, was accepted into the *Dictionnaire de la langue française* published by the Académie Française.

The problem of a formal definition of suicide has been more or less lost sight of between the two problems of how to judge it and how to prevent it. Webster's Third New International Dictionary defines it as "the act or an instance of taking one's own life voluntarily and intentionally." Nothing could be simpler at first glance but then one realizes that a whole range of acts usually considered as suicides does not comply with this definition. If we take the words "taking one's own life" literally, it excludes the cases of Saul, Nero, and all others who asked someone else to kill them. The word "voluntary" would exclude the suicide of Seneca, ordered by Nero, as well as the Japanese hara-kiri, so long as it was compulsory at least for the nobility (until 1868) and the Indian suttee, which occurred under pressure of custom and public opinion. Another difficulty is created by the word "intentionally," of which the meaning is not quite clear. Is it supposed to indicate that the aim of the act is always self-destruction? In that case, what happens in some "heroic" suicides when life is sacrificed to save the life of someone else, to promote a cause, to avenge a disgrace? Should one not rather add to the definition "regardless of the purpose served by one's death"? The French psychiatrist G. Deshaies must have had this in mind when he defined suicide as "an act of killing oneself, usually in a conscious manner, and taking death as a means or as an end."[3]

The heroic and compulsory variants of suicide have become quite exceptional and are therefore of little relevance in defining suicide. A much greater defect in the dictionary definition is, however, that it does not reflect the issue of normal or pathological suicide, or that of conscious and unconscious causes and motives. Deshaies at least takes the latter into consideration when he speaks of the "usually conscious manner." Since both these issues are controversial, one might argue that they do not belong to a definition and that, on the contrary, the real problem of defining suicide is the avoidance of various biases—personal or rooted in theoretical positions. Still, Deshaies's definition seems to be an advance over that given by Emile Durkheim which is still the one most used by sociologists. Durkheim writes that in order to be able to speak of suicide, "it is sufficient that the act from which death must necessarily result has been accomplished by the victim in full knowledge of such an outcome."[4] He points out, however, that the certainty of this knowledge may be greater or less. "Doubtless, a man exposing himself knowingly for another's sake but without the certainty of a fatal result is not a suicide, even if he should die, any more than the daredevil who intentionally toys with death while seeking to avoid it, or the man of apathetic temperament who, having no vital interest in anything, takes no care of health and so imperils it by neglect. Yet these different ways of acting are not radically different from true suicide. They result from similar states of mind, since they also entail mortal risks not unknown to the agent, and the prospect of these is no deterrent; the sole difference is a lesser chance of death. Thus the scholar who dies from excessive devotion to study is currently and not unreasonably said to have killed himself by his labor. All such acts form a sort of embryonic suicide and, though it is not methodologically sound to confuse them with complete and full suicide, their close relationship to it must not be neglected."

These remarks are quoted partly because they also show that what Durkheim calls "embryonic suicide" clearly anticipates what Karl Menninger forty years later called "partial" and "chronic" suicides. While Durkheim cites as an example of excess the labors of a scholar devoted to his studies, the excesses that concern Menninger are alcoholism, drug-taking, and smoking. This may well be taken as a sign of changing times. But while both stress the close relationship of such behavior to suicide, they tend to neglect the important and even crucial differences between these "suicide equivalents" and "the real thing." Neither envisages the possibility that, in many instances, drinking or drug taking may be a defense against suicide, for often people resort to these practices out of motives that drive others to suicide. A person who finds life difficult to bear might, without such "crutches," simply end it. Moreover, most people drink or use drugs in order to "function better" or to have pleasant or "meaningful" experiences—in short, to be more "alive." Thus, although the use and abuse of alcohol and drugs may hasten a person's demise, it does not seem proper to consider such behavior invariably as suicidal. Without in any way underestimating the seriousness of the problems posed by alcoholism and drug addiction, one could maintain that it is the lesser evil to drown one's sorrows in alcohol than to drown oneself, or to go on an LSD trip than to embark on the final "voyage to the end of the night."

11

THE PROBLEM OF "RATIONAL SUICIDE"

The German psychiatrist Alfred Hoche proposed in 1919 the term *"Bilanz-Selbstmord"*—"balance-sheet suicide"—to designate instances where supposedly mentally normal persons dispassionately take stock of their life situation, and having found it unacceptable, if not intolerable, and not anticipating any change for the better, decide to put an end to their lives. A number of prominent European psychiatrists and students of suicide[1] agree with Hoche that such suicides do occur, but some, like Pöldinger, consider them rare and thus without relevance to a discussion of suicide from a medico-preventive point of view.

Actually, there is no way of determining how exceptional balance-sheet suicides are. Only very limited numbers of suicides contact prevention centers, and although many have seen a physician within a few months before they killed themselves, their suicidal inclination remained undetected.

Be it as it may, it would seem proper to distinguish between balance-sheet suicides and rational suicides. "Rational" here implies not only that there is no psychiatric disorder but also that the reasoning of the suicidal person is in no way impaired and that his motives would seem justifiable, or at least "understandable," by the majority of his contemporaries in the same culture or social group.

As far as the thought processes of suicidal people are concerned, Charles Neuringer has found that they are characterized by "rigidity"—that is, inability to find and use new solutions in a crisis.[2] Shneidman and Farberow have shown that "the logical processes of genuinely suicidal people are characterized ... by proneness to commit a particular kind of psychosemantic fallacy" which consists in the "identification between the self as experienced by the self (I_s) and the self as experienced by others (I_o)."[3] This fallacy is due to man's difficulty in imagining his own death (and probably also to the deep-seated belief in immortality) and has the result that one expects to be "alive" and present even after one is dead. Thus suicidal people do not regard killing themselves as "final." But Shneidman and Farberow admit important exceptions to their hypothesis, and Neuringer's study is limited in the number of subjects investigated.

A considerable number of suicides, then, would probably satisfy the requirement of unimpaired logic as a precondition of considering their suicides rational. What distinguishes the latter from balance-sheet suicide more than anything else, however, is the third requirement—approval by contemporaries, in the sense of their agreeing that in similar circumstances they might have done the same thing. Obviously such more "objective" evaluation of the suicidal act varies according to the culture, and even within one cultural setting may change quite rapidly. A Japanese nobleman or officer may commit hara-kiri for reasons which a European or an American in the same situation would not consider sufficient, and therefore neither would view such a suicide as rational. For a European army officer, suicide was *de rigueur* in the nineteenth century if he were unable to pay his gambling debts or had committed some other infraction of the gentleman's code, but today would be considered extravagant even by his peers. Nor is suicide because of a failure in business which had caused the ruin of a number of other people considered rational today, although suicide because of one's own financial ruin may be.

Nevertheless, in all cultures except those that adhere completely to the uncompromising religious condemnation of suicide, circumstances exist which would be judged by the majority as valid reasons for committing suicide. In classical antiquity, as well as in the contemporary Western world, loneliness and isolation of the aged and painful terminal illness have been widely accepted as such mitigating circumstances.

An instance of a contemplated suicide which would certainly pass muster as a rational suicide in all three respects if it had taken place is related by Pliny the Younger, in connection with his friend the eminent lawyer Titus Aristo.

> A few days ago he sent for me and some of his intimate friends, and told us to ask the doctors what the outcome of his illness would be, so that if it was to be fatal he could deliberately put an end to his life, though he would carry on with his struggle if it was only to be long and painful; he owed it to his wife's prayers and his daughter's tears and to us, his friends, not to betray our hopes by a self-inflicted death so long as those hopes were not vain. . . . Many people have this impulse and urge to forestall death, but the ability to examine critically the arguments for dying and to accept or reject the idea of living or not is the mark of a truly great mind. The doctors are in fact reassuring in their promises; it only remains for the gods to confirm these.[4]

The same author provides also the account of a rational

suicide, that of his friend, Corellius Rufus, who suffered from gout which grew worse with advancing age.

> He bore his affliction through sheer strength of mind, even when cruelly tortured by unbelievable agony.... I went to see him in Domitian's time. "Why do you suppose I endure pain like this so long?" he said. "So that I can outlive that robber if only by a single day." When Domitian died he felt free to die too. He broke off all links with life. He refused all food for several days, saying, "I have made up my mind."... He was led to make his decision by the supremacy of reason, which takes the place of inevitability for the philosopher.... He had lived to be sixty-seven.[5]

The issue of rational suicide has particular relevance for a problem of the ethics of suicide prevention. This is the question: "When, if ever, is the clinician willing to say: 'Yes, I agree; it is the best thing for you to do'."[6] Such a question does not arise in connection with balance-sheet suicide, for the simple reason that in most instances the potential suicide's estimate of his situation is probably faulty and thus amenable to correction, but only with rational suicide as defined here. Fortunately, the range is narrow, being limited to cases where suicide is contemplated either for the good of some cause, to save other lives (altruistic suicide), or because of painful terminal illness. In any event, for those engaged in suicide prevention there seems to be no alternative to trying to prevent even a rational suicide, no matter how irrational such a position may be, especially when painful death is inevitable and near.

A particular kind of suicide involving the desire to escape debilitating old age and seek quick and painless death is that of people still in their prime who have decided to end their lives on reaching a certain age. An example of this seemingly classical type of rational suicide is that of Paul Lafargue, Karl Marx's son-in-law. He was a physician by profession but after meeting Marx became active in the socialist movement, took part in the Paris commune in 1871, became a political exile, and after an amnesty returned to France where he was elected to the parliament. On Sunday, November 27, 1911, his gardener discovered the corpses of Dr. Lafargue and his wife in a little pavilion in their garden. He was lying fully dressed on a bed; she was in an easy chair in an adjoining room. Before committing suicide Dr. Lafargue had written out a reference for his domestic help, signed his will, and even drafted the text of a telegram to be sent to his nephew:

> M. & Mme. Lafargue are dead. Come immediately. Doucet, gardener.

In a message to his friends Lafargue wrote:

> Sound of mind and body, I am killing myself before pitiless old age, which gradually deprives me of the pleasures and joys of existence and saps my physical and intellectual forces, will paralyze my energy, break my will power, and turn me into a burden to myself and others. Long ago I have promised myself not to live beyond the age of seventy. I have fixed the moment for my departure from life and I have prepared the method of executing my project: a hypodermic injection of hydrocyanic acid. I die with the supreme joy of having the certitude that in the near future the cause to which I have devoted myself for forty-five years will triumph. Long live Communism! Long live International Socialism! . . .

A report published after his death pointed out as an explanation of his act that Lafargue had in his veins the blood of three oppressed races: his paternal grandmother was a

The Problem of "Rational Suicide"

mulatto, his maternal grandfather was of Jewish origin, and his maternal grandmother was a Caribbean Indian.

There is considerable irony in Lafargue's suicide, for had he waited another six years (and there is no indication that he could not have lived that long), he would have seen the triumph of his cause in Russia in November 1917. In this context, however, the question is whether his suicide should be considered as rational. The same applies to that of Marx's grandson, Jean Longuet, a prominent lawyer, also at the age of seventy, and that of the famous French brain surgeon Thierry de Martell who repeatedly told his colleagues that he would kill himself at the age of sixty-five and did so. How normal is it to plan one's death so far ahead? Is it the height of rationality or is it madness? Even if one opts for the latter, the issue of whether suicide in other types of situations, particularly those involving the torment of dying, should be considered rational is still not resolved.

12

THE PROBLEM OF "EASY DYING"

The idea that suicide may be the most appropriate way of solving the problem of the prolonged and painful dying process to which so many are subjected is by no means new. As far as the individual is concerned, this, like any other suicide, is a matter of personal decision. The question is whether such suicides should not be encouraged and helped as a matter of public policy.

Even to ask this question seems like heresy today when so much effort is being expended in combating suicide. But is not suicide to escape a miserable death entirely different from suicide to escape a miserable life?

In order to consider this issue properly one must separate it from the problem of mercy killing, or euthanasia. Webster's Third New International Dictionary defines euthanasia (from the Greek *eu,* well, and *thanatos,* death) as

> 1. an easy death or means of inducing one; 2. the act or practice of painlessly putting to death persons suffering from incurable conditions or diseases.

The Problem of "Easy Dying"

One should expand the definition by adding either before the word "death" or after the word "means" "physiologically and psychologically," and it is preferable to avoid the term "auto-euthanasia" and to speak instead of "euthanatic suicide." There is a type of euthanasia in which the patient requests to be killed by a physician, nurse, or relative, but this is not suicide in the proper meaning of the word.

The usual arguments against euthanasia do not apply to euthanatic suicide, except perhaps that one may be victim of a false diagnosis or may deprive oneself of the chance that new developments in medicine will bring a cure. But since the patient alone can judge whether he wants or can bear to suffer any longer, even these considerations become of minor importance. The question of euthanatic suicide is then to be judged on its own merits.

The religious opposition to any kind of suicide was discussed earlier. As far as an "easy death" is concerned, it is not what the true Christian primarily aspires to. As the French mathematician and philosopher Blaise Pascal explained in a famous letter to his sister Gilberte, dated October 17, 1651, "The believer has the extraordinary advantage of knowing that in reality death is punishment imposed for having sinned, and necessary for man in order for him to be able to expiate his crime."[1] Thus, for a Christian physical death is not even supposed to be "easy." Christ himself suffered a horrible and painful death. The agony of dying is made easier to bear by the hope of eternal life, but the ordeal must be borne with resignation.

Where religious influence has waned or has been completely eliminated, what arguments against euthanatic suicide can be put forward? Moreover, the arguments in its favor are quite convincing. Thus Seneca writes:

> Whereas a prolonged life is not necessarily better, a prolonged death is necessarily worse. Nowhere should we indulge the soul more than in dying. Let it go as it lists: if it craves the sword or the

noose or some potions that constrict the veins, on with it.[2]

The German philosopher Friedrich Nietzsche (1844-1900) asserts in "The Oldster and Suicide":

> Suicide in this instance is a wholly natural and proper act, which as a victory of reason should justly evoke respect; and it has commended itself in the days when the leading Greek philosophers and the most courageous Roman patriots used to die by their own hand. The mania to keep on vegetating through medical treatment and the most miserable mode of living is much less deserving of respect.[3]

Yet when in 1970 the head of Denmark's Welfare Board renewed the proposal he made some years earlier that people who sincerely intend to commit suicide should be given official help in the form of a pill containing fast-acting and painless poison, the suggestion aroused a storm of protest not only from clergymen but also from politicians and medical spokesmen. This proposal may have some relation to the fact that suicide is considered acceptable in Denmark as a resolution to personal and social tensions. An explanation of why it became acceptable would go a long way toward accounting for the Scandinavian suicide phenomenon—namely that the rate in Denmark and Sweden is around 22 per 100,000, whereas in Norway it is a mere 7.5, even though all three countries are so similar in religion, culture, and social systems, including social services.[4]

That the clergy should denounce the proposal for an officially supplied suicide pill as both "dangerously attractive" and contrary to Christian ethics is understandable. But from frequent practitioners of discreet euthanasia, such protestation "in the name of medical ethics" is not very convincing. Should not the multitudes who die painfully and miserably each year be allowed to decide for themselves what is best for them? Moreover, it would be interesting to ascertain how many among physicians, whose suicide rate is many times that of the average population, are actually euthanatic suicides, due to the discovery of their own terminal illness, their knowledge of how prolonged and painful dying can be, and the easy accessibility of quick-acting lethal drugs.

Once the principle of euthanatic suicide is accepted, the problem of means is easily solved. The official distribution of poison to persons desiring to commit suicide for valid reasons seems to have been practiced in antiquity, in particular on the Greek island of Keos (Kea) and, as mentioned earlier, in ancient Marseilles. On Keos another custom relating to the suicide of old people also seems to have prevailed. The Greek geographer Strabo (63 B.C.-23 A.D.), speaking of the law which helped a person "who was unable to live well to escape from living ill," states that it also provided that persons over sixty years of age were poisoned with hemlock.[5] However, Claudius Aelianus, the Roman historian who "flourished" in the third century A.D., gives a different slant to what seems to have been forced suicide, or outright euthanasia. He reports that "very old men came together, garlanded as if to a banquet, and drank hemlock when they realized that they were incapable of doing anything useful for their fatherland."[6] But while hemlock seems to have been expensive and to have varied in efficacy, today the choice of effective means is practically unlimited.

Making these available for committing euthanatic suicide does not exclude giving the candidates the opportunity to avail themselves of the services of suicide prevention centers before making the final decision. (This might bring into the purview of such centers many intended suicides who otherwise would not come in contact with these facilities.)

The last question is that of the number of people who would use such official help in committing euthanatic suicide. Stengel, who seems rather skeptical in this respect, cites a case of a patient suffering from advanced cancer who repeatedly asked his physician to give him a lethal dose of morphine. But when the doctor inadvertently left a full bottle of the poison at the patient's bedside, he was severely reprimanded by the dying man for his negligence. Several such stories are told and may be true. Even very sick people are ambivalent about death to the last. On the other hand, such occurrences should not be interpreted as confirming the widespread misconception that seriously, even terminally, ill persons are not likely to commit suicide. A great many do and by methods that are not only painful but also dangerous to others.[7]

It would be too much to expect that resistance to the idea of euthanatic suicide will be easily overcome. The most important step in that direction is the realization that considerering suicide the wrong cure for the ills of living does not necessarily exclude the possibility that it may be the right cure for the ills of dying.

13

PHILOSOPHERS ON SUICIDE

Philosophers have at different times rejected, condoned, or advocated suicide, and done so on grounds that were not necessarily philosophical but rather religious, social, or psychological, although their attitudes toward suicide necessarily reflected their views on life and death. But no generalization of any kind is possible in this connection, since even a negative view of life did not always serve as an argument in favor of suicide. Moreover, the belief in immortality does not make death necessarily attractive, and the conviction that death is total annihilation does not always make it an object of terror. Thus we often find that immortalists condemn suicide, and those who think death to be final condone or even recommend it. On the whole, however, philosophers seem to have been instrumental in bringing about the permissive and tolerant view of suicide that generally prevails today. Thanks to them, no one seriously challenges the individual's right to dispose of his life as he sees fit, society does not enforce the penalties which may still be on the books, and even religious sanctions are often waived under some pretext or other. As an indirect result of this humane and enlightened attitude toward suicide, it has become possible to initiate efforts to help the suicidal individual instead of punishing him.

Pythagoras

The attitude toward suicide of the earliest Greek philosphers, those usually termed "Pre-Socratics," is not known, since none of their works survived independently and the quotations from them found in later philosophers make no reference to suicide. The only exception is Pythagoras (born probably in 570 B.C.). According to Plato, he was opposed to suicide, even though he taught that man is a stranger in this world and his soul is in the body as in a tomb.[1] The cause of his prohibition of suicide lies in his doctrine of transmigration of the soul (reincarnation), borrowed from Orphic cults. Being immortal but "fallen," the soul is imprisoned in the body where it undergoes a process of atonement and purification, and on the success of this process depends whether the soul at death will return to its divine origin or transmigrate into another body, to resume or continue its penitential path toward liberation. To interfere with this process by voluntary —that is, premature—death is to revolt against the divine law. One must wait until God releases the soul from its bonds. Thus, even though life is a probation and, as such, clearly acknowledged as an ordeal, suicide is inadmissible.

Plato

Plato (427-347 B.C.) took over from Phythagoras the notion of the immortal and imprisoned soul, as well as the condemnation of suicide. The latter is expressed in the *Phaedo,* when Socrates, who has been condemned to die by drinking hemlock, remarks to his friends, "No man has the right to take his own life, but he must wait until God sends some necessity upon him, as he has now sent upon me."[2]

Plato does not accept the Pythagorean view that life is a penal servitude for sins committed in previous existences and that men have no right to avoid doing penance, but he too considers that man is a "chattel" of God, the way a slave is a "chattel" of his owner, and therefore may not dispose of his own life. This view is binding on the true philosopher, even though he has "the desire for death all his life long."[3] This much misunderstood phrase refers to the Platonic notion that true knowledge is possible only when the soul is free from the body, whose senses are obstacles in the way of discovering "the real." Thus, a person who pursues true knowledge "rehearses" death in the sense that he endeavors to approach in life the ideal state of knowing which can be achieved only after death. He does this by concentrating on his soul and turning away his attention from the body. But this does not imply that the philosopher ought to expedite his death. He, too, must patiently wait until it pleases God to bring about, or decree, the release of the soul.

The reason why one ought not to put an end to one's life ahead of its divinely ordained expiration is that by committing suicide man contradicts God's will, and in doing so forfeits his chance for a pleasant afterlife. Socrates, who firmly believes in the immortality of his "true self," his "soul," expresses the hope that he will find himself after death in the company of the most worthy men of the past.[4] He does so because, among other reasons, he sees his manner of dying not as a suicide but as self-execution, which is only another form of capital punishment, to which he has been condemned, no matter how unjustly, by his judges.

Thus, although for Plato immortality is not a gift of God, but the natural endowment of each and every soul, not all the souls will enjoy the same fate in their future existence because each retains its intrinsic tendencies for good and evil;

Plato even mythologizes about the different lot of the virtuous and the wicked souls.

In any case, Plato thought that suicide ought to be punished by the state, even though he allows some exceptions. In *The Laws* he writes:

> But what of him ... whose violence frustrates the decree of Destiny by self-slaughter though no sentence of the state required this of him, no stress of cruel and inevitable calamity has driven him to the act, and he has been involved in no desperate and intolerable disgrace, the man who thus gives unrighteous sentence against himself from mere poltroonery and unmanly cowardice? Well, in such a case, what further rites must be observed, in the way of purification and ceremonies of burial, it is for Heaven to say; the next of kin should consult the official canonists as well as the laws on the subject, and act according to their direction. But the graves of such as perish thus must, in the first place, be solitary ... further they must be buried ignominiously in waste and nameless spots ... and the tomb shall be marked by neither headstone nor name."[5]

Aristotle

Plato's most outstanding pupil, Aristotle (384-322 B.C.), the only philosopher whose fame and influence at certain periods of history overshadowed Plato's, employed in his quest for knowledge an entirely different principle, that of empirical science, and eventually rejected nearly all of Plato's metaphysics, including especially his theory of eternal "Ideas" and his doctrine of the immortality of the soul. But on suicide he took a position as negative as Plato's. Indeed he was even more uncompromising than his teacher in that he seems to have rejected any exceptions or mitigating circumstances. However, Aristotle in his numerous works devotes to suicide only two brief passages in the fifth book of his treatise on Ethics. The first reference is in connection with the discussion of virtues and vices. He speaks of courage in terms of concern with death, "which is the most terrible of all things; for it is the end, and nothing is thought to be any longer either good or bad for the dead," and defines a brave man as one "who is fearless in face of a noble death" [that is, death in battle] and in "all emergencies that involve death" because of a sense of honor. Then he concludes:

> But to die to escape from poverty or love or anything painful is not the mark of a brave man, but rather a coward; for it is softness to fly from what is troublesome, and such a man endures death not because it is noble but to fly from evil.[6]

The other reference to suicide is in connection with the question "whether a man can treat himself unjustly?" Aristotle writes:

> ... one class of just acts are those acts in accordance with any virtue which are prescribed by the law; e.g. the law does not expressly permit suicide, and what it does not expressly permit, it forbids. Again, when a man in violation of the law harms another (otherwise than in retaliation) voluntarily, he acts unjustly, and a voluntary agent is one who knows both the person he is affecting by his action and the instrument he is using; and he who through anger voluntarily stabs himself does this contrary to the right rule of life, and this the law does not

allow; therefore he is acting unjustly. But towards whom? Surely toward the state, not towards himself. For he suffers voluntarily, but no one is voluntarily treated unjustly. This is also the reason why the state punishes; a certain loss of civil rights attaches to the man who destroys himself, on the ground that he is treating the state unjustly.[7]

The intent of these passages is clear enough. Suicide is a cowardly act. Since it deprives the state of a citizen, it is a crime similar to a soldier's desertion of his post. It is also an amoral act (contrary to the "right rule of life"), and on both accounts should be punished. However, the punishment is not too severe—merely "a certain loss of civil rights." Perhaps Aristotle would not have justified any punishment at all had he taken the more enlightened view that the law does not necessarily forbid what it does not expressly permit.

Curiously enough, when, after the death of his former pupil, Alexander the Great, Aristotle had to flee Athens and soon thereafter suddenly died in exile at the age of sixty-two, there were persistent rumors that he had committed suicide. Their truth, like that of most such stories involving philosophers, is suspect.

Epicurus

The political unrest and spiritual crisis in Athens toward the end of the fourth century B.C. appears to have favored a change in the philosophical outlook on life. In addition to the Platonists, the "Peripatetics" (as the followers of Aristotle were called), and some less important groups like the Cynics and the Cyrenaics, two important new philosophical schools were founded. In 307 B.C. Epicurus (341-270 B.C.), born on the island of Samos of Athenian parents, established his "garden," and in 300 B.C. Zeno of Citium (336-265 B.C.), a Phoenician, began to teach on the "Painted Porch" *(stoa poikile)* and became the founder of Stoicism.

It would be difficult to find two personalities more different than the gentle and gregarious Epicurus and the austere, even ascetic Zeno. No wonder they produced two very different philosophies. But their aim was on the whole the same—to enable man to cope with life's vicissitudes and to come to terms with death.

Epicurus's view of the task of philosophy is expressed in his statement that "vain is the word of that philosopher which does not heal any suffering of man."[8] He taught that the two great afflictions of man are the fear of the gods and the fear of death. The former is unfounded, because, although gods exist, they do not interfere in human affairs. As for the fear of death, this "most terrifying of all ills is nothing to us, since as long as we exist, death is not with us, but when death comes, then we do not exist."[9] Once this is understood, nothing stands in the way of man's happiness, which consists in peace of mind and the health of the body. As long as the latter is unimpaired, life is enjoyable, since bodily pleasure is the highest good, and mental pleasure is derived from and related to it. Epicurus was opposed to suicide, even in misfortune, which "we must heal by the grateful recollection of what has been and by the recognition that it is impossible to make undone what has been done."[10]

While "the many at one moment shun death as the greatest of evils, at another yearn for it as a respite from the evils of life ... the wise man neither seeks to escape life nor fears the cessation of life, for neither does life offend him nor does the absence of life seem to be an evil."[11] Epicurus's negative attitude toward suicide is perhaps best expressed in his sarcastic comments about the statement by the poet Theognis that it is best not to be born but "once born make haste to pass the gates of Death." For, if he really means it, why does he not pass away out of life? For nothing stops him if he really made up his mind to do so. "But if he speaks in jest, his words are idle."[12]

Epicurus's most ardent admirer, the Roman poet Titus Lucretius Carus (99-53 B.C.), the author of the didactic poem *De Rerum Natura* (On the Nature of Things), which is the most comprehensive exposition of materialism in antiquity, and of Epicurean teachings, was less negative toward suicide. But he condemned it if it was committed for the wrong reasons. Denouncing his contemporaries' greed and lust for power, which he attributed to their fear of death, Lucretius is particularly scornful of those who "sacrifice life itself for the sake of statues and titles" and points out that "often from fear of death mortals are gripped by such a hate of living ... that with anguished hearts they do themselves to death. They forget that this very fear is the fountainhead of their troubles."[13] However, those who find no flavor in life should not hesitate to take leave of it. Taking up Epicurus's argument against those who are complaining about the inevitability of death, he asks:

> Why do you weep and wail over death? If the life you have lived till now has been a pleasant thing ... why then, you silly creature, do you not retire as a guest who has had his fill of life and take your carefree rest with a quiet mind? Or, if all your gains have been poured profitless away and life has grown distasteful, why do you seek to swell the total? ... Why not rather make an end of life and labor?[14]

Lucretius himself is supposed to have committed suicide, but although this version of his death is widely accepted, its only source is St. Jerome (born c. A.D. 340). Jerome's source, in turn, was the *Chronicles* of Eusebius of Caesarea (died c. A.D. 325) who, in his report for the year A.D. 95, mentions that "the poet T. Lucretius is born, who later went insane after drinking a love philter, in his lucid moments wrote some books which were amended by Cicero, and who committed suicide at age forty-four."

The Greek Stoics

The decisive change toward approval of suicide was made by Epicurus's great rival, Zeno. While Epicurus accepted the atomism of Democritus but taught that the world is ruled by chance, the Stoic school retained Democritus's doctrine of natural necessity, that the future is inevitably fixed in advance, and that the universe is ruled by divine *logos* (reason), of which man's rational part is a reflection. Thus, to live "according to Nature" is to live according to reason which is a reliable guide to correct action. And while for Epicurus the highest good was pleasure, Zeno proclaimed it to be virtue. The question of suicide, however, is, for the Stoics' "wise man," not one of moral right or wrong, but of a rational decision as to what is preferable in a given situtation, life or death.

Legend has it that Zeno himself committed suicide in his old age. According to one version, when walking along the road he tripped and broke his toe. Interpreting this accident as God's sign that he had lived long enough, he went home and killed himself. Another version has it that he lay on the road holding his breath until he died. His successor, Cleanthes, is also said to have been a suicide. When he developed a boil on his gum he was advised by his physician to refrain from eating for two days. But although his condition improved rapidly and he was told to resume taking normal nourishment, "having gone so far in the path of death, he persisted to the end."[15]

Actually, the stoic position with regard to suicide was in some respects an enlargement of that of Plato. As has been mentioned, Plato allowed exceptions from the general rule in a number of circumstances which were "objectively" intolerable and irremediable. The philosophers of the so-called middle stoa, in particular Panaetius (185-110 B.C.) and Posidonius (135-51 B.C.) replaced objective by subjective criteria, substituting for external compulsion an overwhelming inner conviction. The Stoic who finds it no longer possible to live "according to reason" interprets this as an intimation from God (or "Nature") that it is time to depart from life. This does not mean, however, that suicide should be a rash act resulting from a momentary impulse or a temporary confusion of values; it should be carried out or rejected only after due deliberation. But, as was already indicated, for the Stoic suicide completely lost its moral reprehensiveness; it ceased to be a crime or a sin, and in time the only problem, particularly in imperial Rome, was how to commit it most gracefully and casually, parading one's courage and fortitude.

The Roman Stoics

The most forceful statements of the Stoic position on suicide are those of the Roman Stoics, the wealthy and politically influential Seneca (4 B.C.-A.D. 65) and the former slave, Epictetus (A.D. 50-132). Some typical pronouncements by Seneca, made in one of his famous "Letters to Lucilius," are: "Living is not the good, but living well. The wise man, therefore, lives as long as he should, not as long as he can ... he will always think of life in terms of quality not quantity." More specifically referring to suicide, he says: "Dying early or late is of no relevance, dying well or ill is.... Even if it is true that 'while there is life, there is hope' life is not to be bought at any cost." But Seneca does not believe that one should try to escape the executioner's sword by committing suicide, and he echoes Lucretius's statement that it is folly to die for fear of dying. Yet if one death involves torture and the other is easy and simple, there is no reason why one should not choose the latter. He takes issue with "even professed philosophers who assert that a man may not do violence to his own life, and pronounce it sinful for a man to be his own executioner. We must wait, they say, for the end Nature has decreed. The man who says this does not see that he has blocked his way to freedom. Eternal law has never been more generous than in affording us so many exits to one entry.... The situation of humanity is good in that no one is wretched except by his own fault. If you like, live; if you don't like, you can go back where you came from." And he concludes: "To live by violence is unfair, to die by violence is the fairest of all."[16]

Seneca committed suicide by opening his veins; this, as has been mentioned, was on orders of his former pupil, the emperor Nero, who suspected Seneca of being implicated in a plot to assassinate him. Seneca's wife insisted on dying with her husband but was saved at the last moment at Nero's order.

Epictetus's position was much less radical than that of Seneca. Not only the times had changed. Stoicism having become the dominant philosophy, suicide had become extremely prevalent among the higher ranks of Roman society. A restraining voice was obviously needed, and Epictetus provided it. He was well suited to do so, not being a "radical" like Zeno, or a proud "aristocrat" like Seneca. Aware of the broad interpretation of the justifications for suicide, he warns that suicide for trifling reasons is inadmissible. He presents the problem in an imaginary dialogue with his disciples: "You come saying: 'Epictetus, we can bear no longer to be bound with the fetters of this wretched body, giving it meat and drink and rest and purgation. ... Suffer us to depart to the place whence we came, suffer us to be released from these bonds.' ... Hereupon, I answer: 'Men as you are, wait upon God. When he gives the signal and releases you from your service, then you shall depart to Him.'" And he cites the example of Socrates as showing the only proper attitude.[17]

As has been noted, "departure" for the Stoics must be "reasonable." To make his point, Epictetus compares one's life situation to being in a smoke-filled room. "If only moderately, I will stay; if there is too much smoke, I will go...." However, while emphasizing that one should not be hasty in committing suicide, he also reminds his followers of the consolation which the possibility of suicide offers to suffering humanity.

> To sum up: remember the door is open. Be not a greater coward than the children, but do as they do. When things do not please them, they say, "I will not play anymore." So when things seem to you to reach that point, just say "I will not play anymore" and so depart, instead of staying to make moan.[18]

Montaigne

The permissiveness of ancient philosophers toward suicide was completely obliterated by the uncompromising attitude of the Christian Church, which has already been discussed in some detail. Only after the philosophical thought had regained a modicum of independence from theology with the rediscovery of classical literature which served as a prelude to the Renaissance could a dialogue over suicide be resumed.

The great French essayist Michel de Montaigne (1533-1592) contributed the first significant discussion of suicide to conclude with a decisive departure from the Church's blanket prohibition. He devotes a whole chapter of his *Essays,*

"Custom of the Isle of Cea [Kea]" to the topic of suicide. The title refers to the alleged custom, already mentioned, of making poison available free to all persons who desired to kill themselves and were able to give valid reasons to the court for doing so. Montaigne also mentions, without giving any source, the existence of the same custom in ancient Marseilles.

Montaigne begins by presenting the position of those who hold that there are many situations which are worse than death. He quotes Seneca, one of his favorite philosophers, and describes the Stoic view on suicide and death:

> Death is a very sure haven, which should never be feared, and often sought ... the more voluntary a death is the more beautiful it is. . . . Life depends on the will of others—death on our own will.

As to the religious prohibition of suicide, he argues that "God gives us sufficient dispensation when he puts us in a situation where life becomes worse than death." Referring to the extension of the commandment "Thou shalt not kill" to suicide, he adds, "I don't break the law made for crooks, when I take away my own property—thus I am not obliged to conform to the law made for murderers when I deprive myself of my own life."

Montaigne objected to the idea that one had to ask permission to commit suicide. He considered the act to be foolish, not immoral, but he is very careful to present this view in such a way as not to offend the Church. He therefore proceeds to present the opposite view: We ought not to quit "the worldly garrison" without the express permission of the One who has put us there. When we do so we are deserters who are punished for it in the hereafter. He points out the great doubt which undermines the first position: "Which occasions are sufficient to justify a man in killing himself?" There are many delusions which mislead not only individuals but entire populations into doing away with themselves, whereas one should never give up as long as there is a glimmer of hope. He admits that perhaps there are no inconveniences great enough that one should die in order to escape them. Moreover, no one is capable of determining precisely at what point we ought to give up hope, and he mentions that Pliny considered only a stone in the bladder, and Seneca only "the prolonged disturbance of the soul," as valid reasons to kill oneself. Montaigne also discusses the much-debated question of whether a woman should commit suicide to protect her chastity. On the face of it, he seems to agree with the view that she ought to go to this extreme and cites the canonization of Pelagia and Sophronia. But, typically for him, he cannot refrain from presenting the possible soundness of the opposite view by telling a supposedly true story of a woman who, after having been raped by several soldiers, exclaimed, "Thanks be to God that at least once in my life I was completely sated without having sinned."

Becoming serious again, Montaigne considers instances when one desires death not in order to escape miseries and affliction on this earth but in the hope of a greater bliss in the hereafter. He quotes St. Paul's wish to die in order to be with Christ, pointing out that this shows how erroneous it is to ascribe all suicides to despair.

Only at the very end of the chapter does Montaigne discuss "the custom of Cea." He appears to be in sympathy with it. He concludes his discussion of suicide by saying: *"La douleur insupportable et une pire mort me semblent les plus excusables incitations"* [unbearable pain and a worse death seem to me the most excusable incentives].[19]

Descartes

The negative views of suicide of the French mathematician and philosopher René Descartes (1596-1650) are found in his letters to Princess Elizabeth, the unhappy and neurasthenic daughter of the deposed Elector of the Palatinate.[20] In the letter of October 6, 1645, he touches on the subject of the influence which the knowledge of the immortality of the soul and the happiness which awaits her in the beyond have on those who are bored with earthly existence. He is referring here to those who are not "true" Christians, since he holds that true believers cannot be bored in this life and are certain of immortality. But to seek an escape in suicide is to succumb to the false notion that in this life evil prevails, whereas even in the greatest calamity and most intense discomfort one can always be content if one uses one's reason properly. A more forceful statement against suicide, and the reason for its rejection, are found in the letter of November 3, 1645. Here Descartes modestly disclaims precise knowledge of the state of the soul after it leaves the body at death. He suggests that if we put aside for the moment what religion tells us and rely solely on natural reason, the most rosy expectations will always be mere conjectures, not certainties. However, reason tells us not only that there are more good things in this life than evil ones but also that we should not give up something uncertain. "Thus reason seems to me to teach us that we should not really fear death, but also that we should never seek it."[21]

Descartes evidently realized that his assertion that the good in life outweighs the bad needed some justification. In the letter of January 1646[22] he explained that what he means is that we should attribute little importance to things which do not depend on our own free choice, and that those things which do so depend we can always render good if only we know how to use them properly. Moreover, with the help of reason all the evil that comes our way from the outside can be prevented from causing more sadness than is evoked by watching similar disasters on the stage. Descartes admits, however, that in order to be able to react in this way one has to be a true philosopher. Nevertheless, he holds that even those who let themselves be overwhelmed by their passions still believe in the depths of their souls that there is more good than evil in the world. Even though they may call for death to deliver them when they suffer great pain, they do not really want to die. Those who seriously want to die and kill themselves do so because of an error in judgment, not at all because of considered reasoning. In any case, Nature does not impose negative feelings about life on people, whereas it is natural to prefer the good of this life to its evils.

Spinoza

There is no condemnation of suicide in Spinoza, nor is there advocacy of it. As a matter of fact, he devotes so little space to the subject that one may wonder how a thinker for whom the goal of philosophy was "the attainment of continuous supreme and unending happiness" could have neglected what in many instances appears as the dreadful consequence of unhappiness.

However, what Spinoza does say about self-destruction in general explains his brevity. His position is extremely interesting, particularly when compared with the current views on self-destructive propensities.

> ... No one, I say, from the necessity of his own nature, or otherwise than under compulsion from external causes, shrinks from food or kills himself. ... That a man, from the necessity of his own nature, should endeavor to become non-existent is as impossible as that something should be made out of nothing.[23]

This amounts to no more and no less than a categorical denial of a natural impulse for self-destruction.

This is the direct consequence of the famous principle stated in Proposition VI of the third book of the *Ethics*: "Everything, in so far as it is in itself, endeavours to persist in its own being." [24] As is made clear in proposition VII, this endeavour *(conatus)* for self-preservation is determined from the necessity of the divine nature by which all things exist. This principle, as far as Spinoza is concerned, covers both inanimate objects and animate beings, including man. It is important to realize that the *Conatus in suo esse perseverendi* (the drive to self-preservation) is not an act of free will; Spinoza describes it as the innate love of each person for himself.

The denial of a natural impulse of self-destruction deserves some scrutiny, particularly in view of the present-day tendency to assert the existence of such an impulse as a basic trait of the human psyche; Freud, in his theory of the death "instinct" in all living things, went so far as to endow it with "ontological" status as a cosmic force, "Thanatos," locked in eternal struggle with "Eros."

The principle of self-preservation as a basic law of nature has a long and venerable history. It goes back to the Peripatetic school as well as to the Stoics who held that the animal's first impulse (appetite) is for self-preservation. St. Augustine, St. Thomas Aquinas, and the Scottish theologian Duns Scotus (1265?-1308) reiterated the assertion that every natural thing (everything that exists), desires its own existence, and many Renaissance philosophers variously restated this, so that the principle of self-preservation had become practically a philosophical axiom by the time Spinoza expounded it. His term *"conatus"* had already been used by Cicero as an equivalent of "appetite," both of these being translations of the Greek term $o\rho\mu\acute{\eta}$, and Spinoza equates this term with "force" *(vis)*. Recently the similarity with Freud's "libido," of which *conatus* is asserted to be an ancestor, has been pointed out. There are other similarities between Spinoza's and Freud's psychological views, and as late as 1910 (at the meeting on student suicide already described) Freud wondered "how it becomes possible for the extraordinarily powerful life instinct to be overcome." His subsequent attempt of explanation by stipulating the existence of an equally powerful death instinct is no less "metaphysical" than Spinoza's assertion of the impossibility of a self-destructive "conatus." What makes suicide possible for Spinoza is physical or psychological compulsion, which may be overt or latent but is always "external."

French Eighteenth-Century Philosophers

The eighteenth-century French *philosophes* take, on the whole, a distinctly permissive view of suicide, which ranged, depending on their philosophical position, from unconditional approval to certain reservations based on sociological considerations.

Thus the materialist and atheist Baron Paul Henri Dietrich d'Holbach (1723-1789) unconditionally approves suicide, a view which follows naturally from his idea that death is the supreme remedy for all human ills. Not only is suicide not against nature, it actually carries out nature's verdict. Nature, far from rejecting the suicidal individual, has labored thousands of years to create the very iron which will cut short his years. Nor is suicide a crime against society, since the contract between it and the individual is made for mutual benefit, and therefore if society cannot make life tolerable to the individual, the latter is no longer bound by the contract. Moreover, an unhappy man is a burden to his fellow men, and his voluntary departure a good solution all around.[25]

The deist Voltaire (1694-1778) insists that individual circumstances, not dogma or preconceived ideas and superstition, must decide whether the suicide acted properly or wrongly, praiseworthily or damnably. Typically, he infuses common sense as well as wit and irony into his generally tolerant view of suicide by ridiculing "romantic" suicides and by explaining that his own suicide is very improbable since he is drawing liberal life pensions from two monarchs and would hate to have them benefit from his premature death.

What is new in Voltaire is that he used empirical material—reports of historical suicides as well as contemporary newspaper accounts—in order to draw conclusions about suicide in general. Thus he found that suicide is more frequent in cities than in rural areas. He attributed this to the greater leisure of city dwellers, who have more time to think and therefore are more prone to melancholia. He also thought that suicidal tendencies, like other moral characteristics, are inherited, and that some suicides are due to a desire for revenge.[26] These conclusions were widely accepted by subsequent students of suicide, and although the first three have been discarded in recent times, the motive of revenge has been recognized and even stressed.

Somewhat earlier, Montesquieu (1689-1755) in his *Lettres Persanes* (1721), castigated the barbaric laws against suicide. Usbek, the Oriental voyager who is his imaginary spokesman, ridicules the moral, religious, and legal sanctions imposed on people who kill themselves. He argues that life is a gift, and that once it ceases to give us pleasure we can return it. Suicide does not hurt society, nor does it disturb the beauty and order of the world, since the body is destined to perish in any event, and the soul remains unimpaired.[27]

Surprisingly, Denis Diderot (1713-1784) in his article on "suicide" in the *Encyclopédie* (1765), takes an antisuicide position. He says that it is unnatural, since it goes against the instinct of self-preservation, transgresses the divine law as embodied in the teachings of the Church, and is antisocial. Some have surmised that this reflected, not Diderot's actual opinion, but his desire to avoid trouble with the authorities.

However, Diderot also presents the arguments for the opposing position; probably he simply wanted to present a balanced account in keeping with the scientific spirit of the *Encyclopédie*. He insists that suicide cannot be called a crime if it is committed, as it often is, in the state of insanity or deep depression—*"melancolie noire."*[28] In this assertion he anticipates the position of the French alienists of the nineteenth century. His friend and collaborator, the great mathematician Jean d'Alembert (1717?-1783), was even further ahead of his time in emphasizing particularly the harm suicide did to the survivors.

The Encyclopedists and their circle can be credited with having contributed to the subsequent morally neutral attitude toward suicide and to its recognition as a danger to the mental health of the community, thus preparing the way for present-day efforts toward its prevention.

The most influential statement of a pro-suicide position was made by Rousseau in the twenty-first letter of his novel, *La Nouvelle Héloïse* (1761). Its hero, the young St. Preux, explains to his friend Lord Edouard his reasons for justifying suicide. It is man's natural right to seek what is good for him and flee what is bad, as long as it does no harm to others. But the brunt of the argument is aimed at squaring the right to suicide with the belief in God. Since God has endowed man with reason precisely for the purpose of enabling him to choose what is best for him, man has to listen to it, and reason tells us that an unhappy life must be remedied as much as a sick body: "If it is permitted to seek a cure for gout, why not for life?" Suicide does not alienate us from God and is not a sin, since in killing ourselves we merely destroy our bodies and bring our immortal souls closer to God. If St. Preux had believed differently he would not want to die. He recognizes one restriction only—that people who have duties to others should not commit suicide. As to himself, he is neither a magistrate, nor has he a family to support, so that nothing stands in his way.[29]

Rousseau, whose own life was extremely unhappy, was rumored to have eventually committed suicide, but this seems doubtful. What seems certain, however, is that Rousseau discussed suicide at length with David Hume (1711-1776), the great English philosopher whose ungrateful guest he was in 1766/67.

Hume

Hume's essay "On Suicide" (published only in 1777, a year after his death, and promptly suppressed) is the most forceful and best-reasoned statement in English, and perhaps in any language, of the Enlightenment's position on the subject. He concentrates on refuting the view that suicide is a crime. To be so defined, it must be a transgression of our duty either to God, to our neighbor, or to ourselves. As to the first, he argues that God has established general and immutable laws by which all that makes up the universe is governed. Once this had been done, however, there is no event, no matter how important in the eyes of men, which is exempted from these laws or which He has "particularly reserved for his own immediate action and operation." But as the inanimate parts of creation carry on without regard to men, these in turn are "intrusted with their own judgment and discretion ... and may employ every faculty with which they are endowed, in order to provide for their case, happiness, or preservation." If this is so, "what is the meaning of the principle that a man, who, tired of life, and haunted by pain and misery, bravely overcomes all the natural terrors of death, and makes his escape from this cruel scene ... [is] encroaching on the office of the divine providence, and disturbing the order of the universe?" To assume this is plainly false, because it presupposes that human life has a special value in the scheme of things. But—and here Hume makes the famous assertion which put him into sharp opposition to the traditional religious position—"the life of a man is of no greater importance to the universe than that of an oyster."[30]

This statement is of particular importance for an inquiry into the possible relationship between the denial of a "cosmic" or transcendent meaning of human life and suicide. An argument often advanced is that if human life has no such meaning, it is not worth while, and since such a view may lead to despair and even to suicide, it must be wrong and life must have such an ultimate meaning.

One of the most frequent arguments against suicide compares it to the desertion of the post to which each individual has been assigned by Providence. Hume counters this by questioning the validity of the analogy. He argues that one's birth is due to a long chain of causes, many of which depend upon voluntary actions of men. "Since Providence guided all these causes, and nothing happens without its consent," the same applies to a man's death, even a voluntary one. Hume invokes in this connection the Stoic view that when pain and sorrow gain the upper hand over one's will to live, this may be a clear indication that Providence is recalling us from our post.

Turning to the second aspect, suicide as a crime against society ("one's neighbor"), Hume argues that by committing suicide one does not harm society but merely ceases to do good, which, if an injury at all, is "the lowest kind of injury." In any case, one is not obliged to do a small good to society if this causes great harm to oneself. Moreover, a man tired of life is often a burden to society since he hinders other useful members from being even more useful.

As to the third "criminal" aspect of suicide, transgression against oneself, no one can deny that suicide is often consistent with self-interest, particularly in cases where old age, sickness, and misfortune make life a burden.

Hume concludes by stating his belief that no one throws away his life as long as it is worth keeping and by declaring that "prudence and courage should engage us to rid ourselves at once of existence when it becomes a burden." By following this rule one actually renders a service to society by setting an example which, if followed by all, would preserve man's chance for happiness while making possible release from suffering and misery.

Kant

Immanuel Kant, who devoted most of his efforts to disproving Hume's skepticism, which for him meant the end of philosophy, disagreed also with his position on suicide. Kant's reasons for condemning suicide follow from his view of man as belonging not only to the realm of "phenomena" but also to that of "things in themselves" *(noumena)*, and from the central place "duty" occupies in his ethics. Not surprisingly, it is his discussion of "the duties of man toward himself" that contains his discussion of suicide.[31]

As a natural being, as an "animal creature," man's first duty is self-preservation, and suicide therefore is a vice (which interestingly Kant puts into the same category as gluttony and the "unnatural" exercise of the sex drive, by which he probably meant sexual intercourse not solely devoted to procreation). But man is also a moral being, embodying the dignity of humanity in his person, and his being a person *(Persoenlichkeit)* lays upon him even more strictly the duty of preserving his life. This is the essence of Kant's criticism of the Stoic position on suicide. Since it seems nonsensical that a man can offend himself, the Stoics considered it as superiority in the true philosopher to be able to withdraw from life at his own discretion with a tranquil soul. But, argues Kant, precisely this courage, this inner strength not to fear death and to know something which man can value higher than his life, should serve as an even stronger reason for not destroying a being with powers capable of triumphing over the strongest emotions. In Kant's view, to annihilate the subject of morality in its own person is equivalent to destroying morality itself, to disposing of the moral person, which is an end in itself, as a means for attaining a purpose of one's own choosing. By doing so, man would be degrading the humanity inherent in his person *(homo noumenon)* in whose safekeeping man the phenomenon has been entrusted.

Although Kant's discussion of suicide occupies only a couple of pages, he closes it with some provocative questions: Is heroic suicide (to save one's country) or deliberate martyrdom by sacrificing one's life for the sake of mankind's salvation to be considered suicide? Is it permissible to escape a death sentence by killing oneself, even when a higher authority commands it as Nero did in the case of Seneca? How about a monarch who carries a poison so that in case of his capture he may spare his country the necessity of accepting disadvantageous conditions for his release? Or a person who, bitten by a rabid dog and knowing his condition to be incurable (this was written before Pasteur), kills himself to avoid endangering others? Or someone who accepts a smallpox vaccination and thus risks his life (in Kant's day vaccination was considered unsafe) for the sake of possibly saving it? However, in asking these questions Kant was obviously less concerned with a proper definition of suicide than with the challenge which such suicides, especially those committed for moral reasons, present to his main argument against suicide.

Schopenhauer

The father of modern pessimism, Arthur Schopenhauer (1788-1860), who saw himself as the heir of Kant, occupies a very original position with regard to suicide. Readers of his magnum opus *The World as Will and Idea* (1818) are frequently surprised to find that he does not consider suicide as a logical conclusion to be drawn from his unrelenting and uncompromising indictment of human existence. "Whoever is oppressed with the burden of life, whoever desires life and affirms it, but abhors its torments, such a man has no deliverance to hope from death, and cannot right himself by suicide."[32]

The reason for this view is to be sought in Schopenhauer's metaphysics. Modifying Kant's position that the real reality, the "thing in itself," is unknowable, Schopenhauer asserts that it can be known, and that it discloses itself, through insight into our own real essence, as "Will," a blind, relentless, and universal striving which expresses itself in organic nature, and consequently also in man, as the "will to live." Since, according to Schopenhauer, this will to live is at bottom the source of all our suffering, misery, and pain, salvation can be achieved only by denying it. But this denial is not achieved through dying, since "our true nature, the Will, is indestructible." This is the reason that he says, in order to explain why suicide is not a genuine solution for the human predicament, that "suicide denies only the individual not the species" and "the willful destruction of the single phenomenal existence is a vain and foolish act; for the *thing in itself* remains unaffected by it, even as the rainbow endures, however fast the drops which support it for the moment may change."[33]

Far from being the result of a loss of the will to live, suicide is, on the contrary, "a phenomenon of strong assertion of will ... the suicide wills life, and is only dissatisfied with the conditions under which it presents itself to him. He therefore by no means surrenders the will to live, but only life."[34]

Nevertheless, although he insists that suicide is a vain and foolish act, Schopenhauer vigorously defends the right of every individual to voluntary death. In his *Parerga und Paralipomena* [Odds and Ends] written in 1851, he states: "It is obvious that everyone has no more undeniable right than that to his own personality and life." [35] He suggests that the clergy should be challenged to show by what biblical authority and by what philosophical argument it arrogates to itself the right to brand as a crime an act committed by so many honored and loved people. Is Hamlet's soliloquy, he asks, the meditation of a criminal? And he was incensed by the suppression of the essay in which Hume effectively disposed of the arguments against suicide.

However, Schopenhauer declares that "the only really cogent moral reason against suicide" is that given in his own principal work. This has been outlined in preceding paragraphs, but Schopenhauer himself summed it up thirty years later: "It consists in that suicide is opposed to the achievement of the highest moral goal, in that it substitutes an imaginary deliverance from this vale of tears for the real one."

In general, Schopenhauer says, men put an end to their existence as soon as the terrors of life outweigh the terrors of death. These latter, however, are considerable and stand "like watchmen before the exit door." Perhaps there is no man living who would not have already done away with himself if the end were merely something purely negative, a sudden cessation of existence. Yet there is something "positive" to it, the destruction of the body. And the body shrinks before annihilation precisely because the body is the manifestation of the will to live.

Schopenhauer concludes his brief essay on suicide with the interesting thought that perhaps suicide can be interpreted also as an experiment, a question which man puts to Nature; namely, what change death brings about in man's existence and knowledge. But the suicide wants to obtain the answer by force, which is clumsy and self-defeating, since it eliminates the consciousness which has to receive the answer.

The Italian poet Giacomo Leopardi (1798-1837) was the other outstanding pessimist of the nineteenth century next to Schopenhauer (whose writings he probably did not know). But while Schopenhauer admitted and defended the right of every person to kill himself, Leopardi denies it. In an imaginary dialogue between the Neo-Platonist Plotinus and his disciple Porphyry, he presents the same argument as did Madame de Stael: man ought not to refuse to submit "to that portion of suffering of our race which destiny has appointed to us."[36]

It is interesting that there was actually a discussion of suicide between Plotinus and Porphyry, which the latter recorded and which was quite different from Leopardi's version.

> One day Plotinus noticed that I had the intention of departing this life. He came to me (I lived in his house) and he told me that my desire to commit suicide was not at all reasonable but stemmed from a morbid melancholia, and suggested that I undertake a voyage. I followed his advice and traveled to Sicily. . . . In this manner I was delivered from my craving for death, but this prevented me from staying at Plotinus's side until his death.[37]

Nietzsche

Friedrich Wilhelm Nietzsche (1844-1900), the German philosopher who was influenced by Schopenhauer more than by any other thinker, nevertheless went his own way in many respects, and nowhere as radically as in his opposition to Schopenhauer's denigration of life. "Suffering is no argument against life," he writes to a friend, "and no pain has been able or shall be able to tempt me into giving a false testimony about life as I recognize it."[38]

At the same time Nietzsche was not opposed to suicide:

"The thought of suicide is a strong consolation: it helps to get over many a bad night."[39] The meaning of this cannot be in doubt. For a man who suffered from terrible headaches and recurring blindness which forced him to give up at thirty-two a brilliant academic career, and who knew not only almost constant physical pain but mental torture and abysmal loneliness, the thought that if his condition became unbearable there was always suicide as a way out must be indeed a comforting one.

Other statements make his affirmative position with regard to suicide even more obvious. "Suicide is man's right and privilege," he writes in *The Dawn of Day (Morgenröte)*.[40] He is against interference with suicide. In *Human All-Too-Human* he writes: "Prevention of Suicide: There is a justice according to which we take a man's life, but there is none whatsoever when we deprive him of dying: this is only cruelty."[41] And in *Thus Spake Zarathustra:* "Many die too late, and some die too early. The maxim: die at the right time still sounds foreign to us."[42]

One may see a contradiction between Nietzsche's unconditional, even passionate affirmation of life and his defense of suicide. Psychologically this could be understood as resulting from his ambivalent attitude toward death, which appeared to him sometimes as an enemy and at other times as a friend. In any case, his *"amor fati"*—the acceptance of one's fate—is not compatible with the Dionysian attitude that when such a life becomes impossible one should put an end to it voluntarily, rather than to accept meekly a "living death." Moreover, Nietzsche's world of "Eternal Recurrence" where "all things return eternally, and we ourselves have already been numberless times," is "the world of eternal self-creation and eternal self-destruction."[43] Suicide as a manner of death would seem to conform better to such a world than natural demise, particularly since *all* deaths are conquered by the "eternal return of the same."

Hartmann

Another German, Eduard von Hartmann (1842-1906), author of the once famous and influential *Philosophy of the Unconscious* (1869, English translation 1884), claimed that Schopenhauer's pessimism was not sufficiently well founded. Hartmann did not consider Schopenhauer his teacher but assigned this honor to Kant. Nevertheless there are important similarities between his philosophy and that of Schopenhauer.

Surprisingly enough Hartmann agrees with Gottfried Wilhelm von Leibnitz (1646-1716) that this is the best of all possible worlds. According to Hartmann, it is so because, if a better world were possible, the all-powerful Unconscious would have brought it about. Hartmann sees intelligence and purpose at work, not only in nature but also in history, which, far from being a meaningless change, shows a definite, if not always unhampered, progress toward a definite goal set by the "great Unconscious," which is similar to Schopenhauer's "Will."

But, while this world can be said to be the best possible one, it is not therefore necessarily good, and Hartmann proceeds to demonstrate that life is essentially undesirable. He argues that happiness, toward which everything strives and which is the only discoverable purpose of life, forever eludes man. Life is a continuous disappointment. However, Hartmann does not advocate escape from life. On the contrary, he enjoins man to reconcile himself to life as it is and to give up his illusions that happiness can be attained, either in this world or in the hereafter, since he is not born to be happy but to serve the ends of the Unconscious, which is "cosmic redemption." Although evolution occurs, it only brings with it a multiplication of pains and a heightened sensitivity to them.

Thus, as Hartmann sees it, the redemption of a world doomed to ever-increasing suffering is no more and no less than the extinction of that world.[44]

According to Hartmann, "the principle of absolute teleology" shows that the final aim of all is "the deliverance of the absolute from transcendental misery, and the return to its painless peace by means of the immanent torment of the world evolution.[45] To help in this task is man's supreme duty, since only man's consciousness can make salvation possible. The more consciousness deepens and expands the clearer becomes the discovery that life is essentially evil and futile. With the growth of intelligence and the evolution of mankind, the conviction of this fact is bound to spread and eventually to take possession of all men. Then, by a common act of will, humanity (or a race of supermen that will succeed it on this planet) will decree its own extinction and along with it the disappearance of the world of which man is the consummation. Existence will be "hurled back" into the Unconscious again.

What all this boils down to as far as suicide is concerned is that, instead of seeking escape through individual suicide, man must help in the "suicide" of mankind. The difference between Hartmann and Schopenhauer is that the latter, while considering suicide a "vain and foolish" act, recognized everyone's right to commit it, whereas Hartmann denies this right as going against man's supreme obligation to help God (or "the great Unconscious") to achieve self-deliverance.

Camus

Although not strictly a philosopher in the sense of the other thinkers discussed in this chapter, the French novelist and essayist Albert Camus (1913-1960) deserves special consideration because of his concern with suicide. In the opening sentence of his brilliant essay *The Myth of Sisyphus* (1942), Camus declares that "there is but one truly serious philosophical problem, and that is suicide." What he actually means is that since human life appears to be devoid of meaning (and Camus is convinced that it is), it is not only legitimate but most relevant to ask whether it does not "logically" follow that life is not worth living and therefore suicide the only proper response to life's meaninglessness. His unequivocal answer to this question is that, although life has no meaning, suicide is not justified.

A large part of *The Myth of Sisyphus* is devoted to a description of "the Absurd" and the sources of the feeling of meaninglessness or "absurdity" of life. Camus makes various and often contradictory statements about the Absurd, for which he does not offer a definition since he considers futile any attempt at doing so. But what emerges as the main root of the experience of the Absurd is the conflict between man's moral demands and the world's indifference to them which is what Pascal meant when he complained that it is the "silence" of the infinite expanse of the universe which frightened him. The "most obvious of all absurdities," however, is death, which for Camus is total annihilation. In the final accounting its "bloodstained mathematics" proves the ultimate vanity, the utter meaninglessness, of human existence.

How, then, does Camus justify his rejection of suicide? First he calls attention to the confusion between the statements that life is not worth living and that it is meaningless. It is a mistake to assume that "refusing to grant meaning to life necessarily leads to declaring that it is not worth living. In truth, there is no necessary common measure between these two judgments."[46] The absence of meaning not only does not compel one to commit suicide, but, as Camus asserts, "life will be lived all the better if it has no meaning." To live truly is to be constantly and keenly aware of the Absurd, a state which Camus likens to the state of revolt in which there is a constant confrontation between man and the world he challenges relentlessly. This is the "metaphysical revolt" which despite "the certainty of a crushing fate" avoids "the resignation that ought to accompany it."[47] It is this revolt that gives life its value and confers majesty on it; it is essential "to die unreconciled and not of one's free will" and to preserve to the bitter end one's integrity, and one's pride "the sight of which is unequaled."[48] This appeal to human pride is what, in the end, Camus opposes to the temptation of suicide. Here Camus clearly shows the influence of Nietzsche. Nihilism does not lead to despair but on the contrary is transformed into a proud stance of defiance and triumph over man's fate. In *Nuptials,* a collection of essays written a year before *The Myth of Sisyphus,* he celebrates the joys of life which made it worth living. As Philip Thody correctly points out, in his book on Camus, "it is because Camus, unlike Kafka, Kierkegaard and Sartre, feels instinctively that although the world may at times appear indifferent and strange, he is basically at home in it on the physical plane, that all his logic leads to a rejection of suicide.[49]

Obviously, the mere appeal to human pride and the reference to the joys of life might have little effect on one who finds life unbearable, feels defeated by it, in short is convinced that it is not worth the trouble. But Camus's question whether the awareness of the absurdity of life is "an invitation to death," to which he gives a negative answer, evokes the related question of whether the conviction that life has no meaning is a factor in suicide.

14

SUICIDE AND THE MEANING OF LIFE

Whatever the motives and causes of suicidal behavior may be in a given case, people who contemplate, attempt, or carry out the act of killing themselves often complain that their lives have lost meaning or are no longer worth living. These statements presuppose that their lives did have meaning or were felt to be worth living until certain events brought on a radical change. In the late 1930s the Austrian psychologist Margarete von Andics, a disciple of Alfred Adler, interviewed 100 survivors of attempted suicides at the Vienna Clinic of Psychiatry and Neurology with the view of determining what human beings take to be the meaning of life, or, put negatively, in what circumstances does a person consider that life is meaningless? What is the "thing" without which one does not desire to live any longer?[1] Beginning appropriately with an analysis of what "life" in the biographical meaning of the word consists of, she distinguishes two "spheres." The "personal sphere" comprises childhood and parental home; society, friendship and exchange of ideas; love, marriage, home;

family and relatives; reputation and esteem. The "material sphere" consists of possessions, control of body (health, sexuality, ability to work), talents and school, profession and achievements.

Impeded satisfaction in one or the other sphere assumes the character of deprivation and can become a motive for suicide by making life appear meaningless or intolerable. In particular, a childhood devoid of affection can be said to create a predisposition to suicide. Loneliness, the lack of someone to whom one can unburden oneself, is one of the latent ills in most of those lives which turn to suicide. But Andics attaches the greatest importance to the fact that none of the persons examined by her belonged, at the time of the attempt to commit suicide, to any community of a wider scope than family, love affair, or friendship.[2] She found that the "thing" without which life becomes meaningless was not necessarily "someone" but most prominently a "something" in the form of integration and participation in a larger social context. She quotes Rabindranath Tagore as saying: "He who does not help turn the wheel of the world lives in vain." In other words, in order to feel that his existence has a meaning "the individual must have a part in the practical and surrounding world." She summarizes the results of her study by saying that "despite all individual differences the achievement, or to quote Adler, the 'contribution,' offered to humanity is in the foreground of all statements."[3]

In evaluating this interesting study it is necessary to consider first of all the limitation imposed by its method. Andics assumes that the account which the victim of a failed or frustrated suicidal act furnishes of his life situation corresponds to the thoughts and feelings immediately preceding this act and thus reflects them faithfully. But this is not necessarily true. She herself emphasizes that she is not concerned with the unconscious genesis but only with the phenomenology of the experience, but this self-imposed limitation further diminishes the value of her material. Another criticism concerns the neglect of psychological factors. When speaking of isolation, she does not pay sufficient attention to the fact that it may have occurred, not because of external reasons, but because an individual severs his connection with a wider social sphere because of anxiety, depression, or other internal causes. In other words, the possibility of psychopathology receives short shrift. While she is careful to indicate that her research is concerned only with psychology and not with clinic-psychiatric aspects of her cases, in general she simplifies the motivation of suicide, which is much more complex than her study makes it appear.

A further shortcoming of her study is the narrow social stratum from which her material is derived. All the subjects were economically deprived, and thus it should not be surprising that, in 87 out of her 100 cases material factors decisively contributed to the suicidal intent, leading her to the conclusion that "material difficulty was the most frequent motive for suicide." But she emphasizes that not poverty as such but "chiefly the uncertainty and lack of aim for the future as well as the impossibility of seeing any way ahead . . . that took the ground from under the person's feet."[4]

Of particular interest in Andics' study, as far as the relation of suicide to the meaning of life is concerned, is that what appears as the meaning of life coincides with what makes life worth living. In other words, she and her subjects are considering the meaning or meanings *in* life, and there is no reference whatsoever to the meaning of life "as such," or the "ultimate" meaning of life. This may be partly because her group of subjects did not include intellectuals or persons inclined to speculate about the ultimate meaning of life in general, and partly because the formulation of her question—"In what *circumstances* does life appear meaningless?"—precluded consideration of a correlation between suicide and the meaning of life in general.

In his article, "Life, the Meaning and Value of," in the *Encyclopedia of Philosophy*, the *Encyclopedia*'s editor, Paul

Edwards discusses the "meanings of the meaning of life" and distinguishes between the meaning of life in the "terrestrial sense" and the meaning of life in the "cosmic sense,"[5] which corresponds roughly to what I called in a previous work[6] the "human" meaning and the "ultimate" or "transcendent" meaning, that is, one related to "ultimate reality" of some philosophers or to a personal God. The term "cosmic" does not, however, express the latter referents of the meaning of life, in particular that asserted by religious thinkers, which is based on the assumption of a special relationship of men to God and consists in man's participation in a divine plan which does not necessarily include the "cosmos," but the "dwelling with God" of man's immortal soul. As to the term "terrestrial," it obscures the "idealistic" nature of some of the goals and purposes which constitute the meanings of life in the "human" sense, or more precisely, of the meanings *in* life.

In *The Myth of Sisyphus*, Camus is asking whether there is a correlation between suicide and the conviction that life as such is meaningless. He writes: "One kills oneself because life is not worth living; that is certainly a truth, yet an unfruitful one because it is a truism. But does that insult to existence come from the fact that it has no meaning?"[7] In other words, do people ever commit suicide because they become convinced—as Camus himself was—that life is "absurd," "a tale told by an idiot . . . signifying nothing"?

In one of the last chapters of *Anna Karenina*, Leo Tolstoy describes how the conclusion that life is meaningless brings his hero to the verge of suicide. Levin is led to examine his basic views on life and death when faced with the imminent death of his brother.

> The question which presented itself to him was this: "If I do not accept the answer which Christianity offers, what answers do I believe in? . . . In infinite time, in infinite space, there emerges a bubble-organism, and like a soap bubble it will last for a brief

Suicide and the Meaning of Life

moment and burst, and this bubble is me.... It was a tormenting untruth but it was, nevertheless, the only result of the ceaseless labors of man's reflection in this matter.... It was not only an untruth, it was also a cruel joke by some evil force, and one must resist, escape this force.... And the liberation from it was in the hands of everyone, and this was death." And the happily married, healthy family man Levin was several times so close to suicide that he hid the rope in order not to hang himself and was afraid to go hunting in order not to shoot himself. But Levin did not hang himself, and did not shoot himself, but went on living.

This episode is autobiographical. Since neither Levin nor Tolstoy did actually commit suicide, it is not certain whether Tolstoy believed that despair over life's futility can actually drive anyone to it. Moreover, he notes Levin's surprise that the overwhelming majority of people in his social and age groups, who, like himself, had lost their old beliefs and undoubtedly shared the new, distressing outlook, apparently remained completely unaffected. On the other hand, since Tolstoy came close to suicide several times, he must have felt that there is definitely such a possibility and that some people so deeply disturbed by the realization of life's meaninglessness may in fact kill themselves.

Some writers and students of suicide, among them the American psychologist and philosopher William James (1842-1910), definitely think that such a conviction may be a factor in suicide. James dealt with the topic of the meaning of life and suicide in a famous address to the Harvard Young Men's Christian Association entitled "Is Life Worth Living?"[8] He admits that instances of "metaphysical *taedium vitae* peculiar to reflective men" and "the melancholy and *Weltschmerz* bred of reflection" are in the minority compared to those whose "suicide is the result of insanity or sudden frenzied impulse." Nevertheless, "the plainest intellectual integrity—nay, more, the simplest manliness and honor, forbid us to forget their case." James does not deny that pessimism, or what he calls "the nightmare view of life," has organic causes, and that it does indeed often depend on the subject's liver." But it has also "reflective sources," the principal of which has been "at all times the contradiction between the phenomena of nature and the craving of the heart to believe that behind nature there is a spirit whose expression nature is." It is noteworthy that this contradiction was singled out by Camus forty-five years later (in *The Myth of Sisyphus*) as being at the root of the feeling of the "Absurd." The similarity becomes even greater when we read in James that "there gradually steals over us, instead of the old warm notion of a man-loving Deity, that of an awful power that neither hates nor loves, but rolls all things together meaninglessly to a common doom."

According to James there are several ways to counteract this "speculative melancholy." One can fall back on the "instinctive springs of vitality that respond healthily when the burden of metaphysical ... responsibility rolls off." The thought that one can always escape through suicide is also a great help: "Meanwhile we can always stand it for twenty-four hours longer, if only to see what tomorrow's paper will contain or what the next postman will bring." Finally, it may help to be reminded of the possibility of doing something "about the evils that make his heart sick," and "a challenge of this sort, with proper designation of detail is one that need only to be made to be accepted by men whose normal instincts are not decayed." In short, "mere instinctive curiosity, pugnacity and honor may make life on a purely naturalistic basis seem worth living from day to day to men who have cast away all metaphysics in order to get rid of hypochondria but who are resolved to owe nothing as yet to religion and its positive gifts." But these methods do not work in all cases. Something else is needed, and this is faith in the ultimate meaning of life. "Probably to everyone of us here the most adverse life would seem well worth living, if we only could be certain that our bravery and patience with it were terminating and eventuating and bearing fruit somewhere in an unseen spiritual world." But how can we be certain of this? James frankly admits the bankruptcy of "natural religion naively and simply taken" and realizes that "the times are gone forever when Leibnitzes with their heads buried in monstrous wigs could compose Theodicies." He offers instead something similar to Pascal's "wager": We can either surrender to the nightmare view of life and crown it with our suicide, or we can take the opposite view based on faith in an unseen world and verify our belief in its existence by acting as if it were true—that is, deciding that life is worth living. In order to sway us toward the latter choice James argues that he does not see "why the very existence of an invisible world may not in part depend on the personal response which any one of us may make to the religious appeal. God himself, in short, may draw vital strength ... from our fidelity." And he concludes: "Believe that life is worth living, and your belief will help to create the fact."

This last sentence has often been misunderstood. What James really means is: believe that life has an ultimate meaning and this will make even the most miserable existence seem worth living. James is not concerned with those "whose instincts are not decayed" and whose life is not beset with adversity; for them life will appear worth living regardless of whether or not they are sure that it has an ultimate meaning, and they probably do not even care whether it has one or not. James speaks only to those who are afflicted, as he himself was for a time, by "metaphysical melancholy"—in short, to those to whom life will be worth living only on condition that it partakes of a meaningful scheme of things which extends beyond and above man's brief and wretched earthly existence.

Among contemporaries, the German Catholic theologian

Georg Siegmund, one of whose works is a book on suicide entitled *Sein oder Nichtsein* [To Be or Not to Be],[9] holds that the conviction of the meaninglessness of life frequently causes suicide. In another work he cites the case of a young intellectual, Alfred Seidel, whose suicide was "the last unavoidable consequence of the denial of any meaning to life as is made clear by his posthumous work," and boldly asserts that "innumerable individuals similarly take the fatal step for the same reason without leaving a literary testimonial to it."[10]

To support his contention that only religious faith can give life a meaning and thus prevent suicide, Siegmund mentions Tolstoy, who, according to him, was saved from killing himself because he eventually arrived at his own version of Christianity. He also quotes an episode from Alexander Popowski's biography of the great Russian scientist Ivan Pavlov (1849-1936). An assistant of Pavlov, visibly tormented by religious doubts, asked the famous psychologist whether he thought that God exists. When Pavlov replied that he should read more books on biology, for then he would not need God, the assistant shot himself.

These two instances are obviously not sufficient to establish Siegmund's thesis. especially since he makes no reference to any other factors which may have contributed to suicide. In any event, the two cases he cites are a far cry from "innumerable individuals." Nevertheless the possibility that a conviction of the meaninglessness of life may be a factor in suicide cannot be lightly dismissed.

A leading student of suicide, Erwin Ringel, made a study of the "Value-Experience of Suicides,"[11] in which he maintains that there is a pronounced causal relationship between disturbed experiencing of values and suicide. The disturbance consists in the lack of commitment to "objective" values and the predominance of subjective value judgments characterized by the position "right is what is useful to me." Such disturbance increases the danger of suicide because it leads to the devaluation of life and the weakening of the ability to master one's aggressive tendencies, promotes antisocial behavior, and diminishes the sense of one's own worth. To test his thesis he carried out a study of 100 survivors of suicide attempts. He realizes the pitfall of using such subjects, since the attempt itself may lead to a marked correction in the attitude to values. He argues, however, that if the disturbance is still found after the suicide attempt, it must have been even greater before it. Another difficulty is the multitude of values, and therefore Ringel makes a selection. He leaves out objects of primitive instinct satisfaction and deals with such "things" as human community (family, marriage, children, politics), profession, art (literature and music), religion, science and sports. The attitude toward religion is particularly important here. As is to be expected, Ringel finds a significant deviation among his subjects. They are more disappointed in religion and also more ambivalent about it than the norm. He concludes that suicide forces man to come to grips with the question of life's meaning but points out that religion can become a suicide-inhibiting factor only if it is embraced wholeheartedly, a condition that is difficult to verify.

The problem of the correlation between the question of the meaning of life and suicide is further pursued by Ringel in his article "On Suicide Attempts of Juveniles,"[12] based on a study of 136 female patients. He divides them into four diagnostic groups: debilitated (14), psychopathic (34), neurotic reaction—"cry for help" (49), and an unnamed group (39). It is the last group which he finds most interesting and which is most relevant here. They all were examples of "existential emptiness," a term Ringel borrows from the founder of "Logotherapy," Victor Frankl. Frankl, who postulates a basic "will-to-meaning" nevertheless holds that "the question of the meaning of life as such is meaningless, because it refers to the vague "life in general" and not to a concrete 'specifically mine' existence.[13] For Frankl the term "meaning of life" evidently signifies not some ultimate meaning but a meaningful employment of one's life. His "will-to-meaning" is reminiscent of Pavlov's "goal-reflex." Ringel, however, is not satisfied with the mere statement of the presence of such a condition. He wants to go beyond Nietzsche's statement "those who have a 'why' to live will bear almost any 'how,' "[14] and wants to know why these people have no "why." (Ringel seems to assume, though without sufficient justification, that Nietzsche's "why" refers to the ultimate meaning of life.)

Ringel's answer is that "to everyone there is assigned a role in this world, into which he has to grow, which he has to fill." Ringel emphasizes that "of decisive importance for one's assent to this role are already the very first years of one's life. In this period the child becomes acquainted with his task, and is either encouraged or discouraged in his relation to it. The most encouraging factor here is love which is given the child."[15] What Ringel has in mind is Erikson's "basic trust" *(Urvertrauen)* and he agrees with Schultz-Hencke that "whoever cannot tenderly love the world, whoever was never capable of establishing this special nearness to anyone, is essentially unfit for life and will, at some time or other, refuse life."[16]

The statement that everyone has his role in the world assigned to him is problematic; unless it is meant in the religious sense it is obviously gratuitous.

But what about the problem of the meaning of life as such? There are those who hold that to ask this question is a sign of "sickness." Thus, in a letter which Freud wrote two years before his death to his French disciple and friend, Princess Marie Bonaparte, on August 1937,[17] he remarks:

> The moment one inquires about the sense or value of life one is sick, since objectively neither of them has any existence. In doing so one is only admitting a surplus of unsatisfied libido, and then something else must happen, a sort of fermenting, for it to lead to grief and depression.

But he adds, "These explanations of mine are certainly not a grand scale, perhaps because I am too pessimistic." Unfortunately, it is not at all clear whether Freud's phrase "the sense of life" refers to the ultimate meaning of life of which Tolstoy, James, and others speak, rather than to meanings that people usually find in their daily lives. Assuming that he is referring to the former, and this assumption seems justified since Freud began his letter with the reference to his approaching death and his disbelief in immortality, certainly this question is asked or arises in unusual circumstances, but is it for all that necessarily "pathological"?

Jung considers a search for the meaning of life a central problem of the emotionally maladjusted and declares that "among all my patients in the second half of life—that is to say over 35—there has been not one whose problem in the last resort was not that of finding a religious outlook on life." [18] Frankl seems to take a similar position when he states that "a doctor should never confuse that which is human with that which is pathological or even confuse with something abnormal which is the most human of all. Man's will-to-meaning represents the most human phenomenon possible, and its frustration does not signify something pathological, at least not in itself. A person is not necessarily sick if he thinks that his existence is meaningless."[19] But Frankl, as was noted earlier, does not speak of the ultimate meaning of life, since he considers the question of the meaning of "life as such" meaningless.

In this respect he (like Freud, who by branding this question as pathological also dismisses it as a pseudo-problem) is at one with an influential school of contemporary philosophy, the so-called Neo-Positivists. They consider the problem to belong to religion, mysticism, and poetry rather than to "serious"—that is, scientifically oriented—philosophy, since it cannot be answered in the same way as scientific questions like "What is the size of the moon," "What is the weight of this table?" One can argue, of course, that the assertion that the question of life's meaning is not "legitimate" is based on an arbitrary definition of philosophy. More importantly, as Adam Schaff has pointed out,[20] to call a problem a "pseudo-problem" does not make it disappear. Schaff, a leading Polish Marxist philosopher, has called attention to the neglect of the problem of life's meaning in Marxism and tries to give a "Marxist" answer to this question—namely, "we want on earth a happy life."

"Legitimate" or not, it must be admitted that the problem of life's meaning has been haunting man ever since he was able to reflect about the world and himself. It may be useful to consider the occasions on which this question arises. It presents itself first of all in the purely theoretical reflections on man's place in the universe and on the fragility, brevity, and transitoriness of human life, which have been expressed by practically all the great writers and poets. More importantly, this question almost inevitably enters people's minds when reverses and disappointments, pain and suffering, become part of their own experience, and particularly when they come face to face with death, their own or that of their loved ones. Why all this suffering and heartache? What is the purpose of all this struggle and striving if in the end one disappears into nothingness?

There is no reason whatsoever to dismiss this question as illegitimate or pathological. As a matter of fact, there are good reasons for considering it the most important question man can ask himself and the most urgent question for philosophers today, because the two-thousand-year-old religious answer has now become unacceptable to an ever-growing number of people. Yet not only do most contemporary philosophers neglect the problem or dismiss it, but throughout the history of philosophy, only a few thinkers have specifically considered it, and none has made it the central object of his reflection. Of those who have considered it, several have arrived at the conclusion that life has no meaning at all, or at best only such meaning as man himself can give to his brief moment on this earth.

Suicide and the Meaning of Life

One can argue successfully with those who take the view that the negative aspects of life far outweigh the positive. However, when one deals with the question of man's "destiny" as an individual and as a species, the pessimistic position is not easily refuted unless one is able and willing to embrace the religious position. This is bad news in our secularized times if indeed people do commit suicide because they believe that life has no meaning. In such a situation it must seem a relief to be told that to ask the question of the meaning of life one must be sick, for then there is at least hope of a cure.

How important in preventing suicide is a positive answer to the question of the ultimate meaning of life? If the importance is measured in terms of people who do commit suicide because they become convinced that life has no such meaning it is not very great, if it is relevant at all, since there is no clear-cut evidence that, even in the few instances where it is claimed by the suicide to be the decisive factor for his act, other factors and some degree of pathology do not enter. Although to ask the question of the ultimate meaning of life is not in itself pathological, and many perfectly normal people ask it much more often than is usually assumed, to kill oneself when one is unable to find a positive answer does not seem to be a "normal" reaction. Many suicides, however, are committed because life has lost its meaning in the "human" or "terrestrial" sense—that is, when someone or something that gave a "meaning" to a person's life has been lost. The question which remains open and which requires empirical evidence, is whether the conviction that life has an ultimate meaning is instrumental in mitigating the despair brought on by such a loss. This is in a way the same question as whether "religion" helps to reduce the danger of suicide but with the important difference that the answer to the ultimate meaning of life does not have to be sought within the confines of tradiditonal religious faiths. Whether it can be found outside of these may well be the most crucial issue facing contemporary man.

CONCLUSION

SUICIDE IN PERSPECTIVE

The preceding chapters have sufficiently emphasized the seriousness of suicide as a mental-health problem and its complexity as a sociopsychological phenomenon. However, it would be a serious omission not to look at suicide in a broader perspective and to question some of the assertions accepted as indisputable by most students of suicide.

In the following paragraphs, suicide will be considered in relation to the population as a whole, to the totality of deaths from all causes, and, finally, to the fact that dying is often a protracted and cruel ordeal.

The first two of these perspectives were touched on in connection with statistical data on suicide. Officially more than 20,000 persons, unofficially possibly more than 30,000 commit suicide in the United States each year. These are impressive, even frightening figures. Yet one should beware of losing one's perspective and sense of proportion, or worse, unnecessarily distorting it for whatever worthy purpose. The true state of affairs is definitely falsified when, in order to emphasize the magnitude of the problem, one invokes the image of a city of 25,000 to 30,000 population being wiped out each year by suicide. A much more correct analogy would be that of a city of 100,000 population in which only one person per month takes his own life. (The actual number is even smaller since the rate is not 12 but 11 per 100,000.) If the population of such a city is viewed realistically, with all its daily problems of gaining a livelihood, the tensions, anxieties, worries and quarrels, marital conflicts, financial hardships, sickness, bereavement, indifference, animosity, and so on, and observe that only one person out of 100,000 on one day out of thirty decides that he had enough of what we all agree to call "the rat race" and kills himself, one might begin to wonder not why he did so, but why it was only he out of so many who reached this decision.

Regardless of whether one considers the rate of 11 per 100,000 "understandable" or still inadmissibly high, it will also help one to see suicide in the proper perspective in relation to the population as a whole if one translates the rate into percentages and realizes that it is equivalent to slightly more than 0.001 percent of the total population. Expressing the incidence of suicide in these terms contributes also to a critical attitude toward the assertion that suicide is a reliable indicator of the mental malaise of a nation or a "barometer" of its social tensions, since it allows one to compare the figure for suicide with that for the emotionally disturbed, which, according to a recent broad consensus, is no less than 10 percent. Yet the former percentage is far from indicating the size of the latter.

Those who hold that incidence of suicide does reveal the poor state of mental health of a given population will argue that completed suicide is like the visible top of an iceberg, the last stage of various kinds of self-destructive behaviors and "suicide equivalents." But it is precisely this view of suicide that is challenged by the relative insignificance of the number of suicides, which points rather to the probability that taking one's life is something radically different from all other life-endangering activities, many of which an unbiased analysis might show to be defenses against the last desperate step.

The relatively small number of suicidal people compared to the overall population throws considerable doubt also on the theory of the existence of a distinct self-destructive tendency in man. The highest estimate of still-living suicide attempters in the United States—between 5 million and 7 million—is still only 2.5 to 3 percent of the total population, and of these no more than 10 to 25 percent at most will attempt suicide again. And although practically everyone at one time or another has toyed with the idea of killing himself, one nevertheless cannot overlook the fact that, while so many have thought of it, relatively few actually commit or even attempt suicide.

The second perspective in which suicide ought to be considered is that of the totality of death from all causes. Suicide is ranked tenth or eleventh for the total population, third in the 15-24 age group, and fourth in the 25-44 group. But such information is misleading, since it does not show that numerically suicides represent little more than 1 percent of all yearly deaths. There were, according to the U.S. Bureau of Census figures for 1966, 21,281 suicides as compared to a total of 1,863,149 deaths from all causes. The breakdown of causes is as follows: "major cardiovascular-renal diseases," 1,021,188; "malignant neoplasm, 303,736; "influenza and pneumonia," 63,615; "diabetes mellitus," 34,597; and "cirrhosis of the liver," 26,692; diseases of early infancy 51,644; non-motor-vehicle accidents, 60,522; motor-vehicle accidents, 53,041; suicide, 21,281.[1] To put it differently, although suicide ranks among the first ten causes of death its rate per 100,000 population was approximately 11 (10.9) in 1966 and 11.1 in 1965, whereas that from cardiovascular diseases was 521.4 and that of cancer (malignant neoplasm) 155.1, or respectively fifty and fifteen times greater.

In the age group 15-24 where suicides rank as the third

cause of death, there is also a considerable numerical gap between suicide and other causes. Statistics for 1963 show the number of all deaths in this age group as 29,321. Of these 15,889 were due to accidents, 2,334 to cancer, and 1,663 to suicide.[2] Though less dramatic than in the total population, the numerical gap is still considerable: suicide represents less than 6 percent of all deaths among the young. While this figure does not take into account the probability that at least some of the deaths recorded as accidents were actually suicides, suicide is still numerically so far inferior to the first two causes, that to speak of it as "the third cause of death" is misleading unless the actual figures are given.

These observations should not be interpreted as an attempt to minimize the importance of trying to understand suicide and reduce its occurrence. As Shneidman points out, suicides are "unnecessary"—that is, preventable—deaths. Moreover, they are the most disturbing ones, not only because of their disastrous and lasting effect on the survivors, but because, especially when they occur among the young, they frequently eliminate potentially valuable members of the community.

However, the recent emphasis on suicide prevention should not obscure the fact that suicide is not always the worst solution. There are situations in which life should not be given priority. One can even go a step further and maintain that not every kind of life should be deemed acceptable. As far as the latter issue is concerned, opinions will differ as to what a "good" life is. Although establishing the minimum requirements for judging life to be worth living will always present a problem, there probably will be a consensus in cases when debilitating disease threatens to turn a human being into a "vegetable" or when a slow and painful dying process sets in.

This leads to the last of the three perspectives in which suicide should be viewed, that of its relationship to death as man's universal lot. It has often been said that to be killed or to kill oneself is the easiest manner of leaving this world. What this means is that these are the quickest and least painful ways of dying, assuming of course that death is achieved expertly and "properly."

If would seem, therefore, that perhaps suicide as a manner of dying ought not to be ruled out. One step in this direction would be the removal of the stigma still widely attached to suicide, a task which suicidologists also consider to be of great importance, albeit for different reasons. In any case there is much to be said for the view of suicide as man's proud privilege, which, according to Pliny the Elder, elevates him above the gods who cannot choose death even if they want to: "But the chief consolation for nature's imperfection in the case of man is that not even for Deity are all things possible—for he cannot, even if he wishes, commit suicide, the supreme boon bestowed on man among all the penalties of life."[3]

It is obvious that this privilege ought not to be abused. But neither should there be undue restrictions on the uniquely human capability to reject an unwanted existence, since it gives man mastery not only over his life but to some extent also over his death.

APPENDIX
REFERENCE NOTES
INDEX

APPENDIX

ASSESSMENT OF SUICIDAL POTENTIAL

One of the most important problems in suicide prevention is the correct evaluation of the suicidal risk of a patient (his "suicidality"). Walter Pöldinger has evolved a list which differs from previous ones in that it emphasizes the *combination* of psychopathologic, psychodynamic, and sociological factors found in suicidal people. The most important factors are listed vertically on the left, numbered 1-35. These numbers are repeated horizontally in a single line at the top and those which apply to the case being evaluated are circled.

The figures 0, 1, or 2 which appear on the point at which the lines intersect measure the frequency of the simultaneous appearance of both factors in a suicidal patient (based on empirical data of Pöldinger, Paul Kielholz, and Erwin Ringel); 0 designates no or only a slight correlation, 1 a definite correlation, and 2 a very high correlation. Where coordinates cross in a given case the figure is circled; these figures are added together and the total for each line given on the right. The sum total at the bottom of the right-hand column is the measure of the suicidal risk. A total of over 100 indicates very high risk, 50 to 100 less but still significant suicidality, and under 50 a very slight risk.

The example reproduced on the next two pages is a risk list of a female patient who subsequently committed suicide.

LIST TO EVALUATE THE RISK

		1	②	3	④	5	⑥	7	8	⑨	⑩	⑪	12	⑬	14	⑮	⑯	17	⑱	⑲
1	Male	0	0	0	0	0	2	1	1	1	2	2	1	1	1	2	2	2		
2	Female	0	⓪	0	⓪	1	2	①	②	②	1	①	2	②	②	0	②	②		
3	Under 45			0	0	1	2	0	1	1	1	1	0	1	2	1	2	2		
4	Over 45				0	⓪	1	2	①	①	①	1	①	1	①	②	1	②	②	
5	Single								1	2	1	1	1	1	1	1	1	1	2	2
6	Married								①	②	①	1	①	0	①	①	0	②	②	
7	Widowed								1	1	1	1	1	1	1	1	1	1	2	2
8	Divorced/separated								1	1	1	1	1	1	1	1	1	1	2	2
9	No religious affiliation									②	②	0	⓪	2	①	①	1	②	①	
10	Family difficulties									②	2	②	1	②	②	2	②	②		
11	Love-marriage-sex problems										2	②	2	②	②	2	②	②		
12	Occupational difficulties											2	2	2	2	2	2	2		
13	Financial difficulties												2	①	①	1	②	②		
14	Sickness/chronic pain													2	2	1	2	2		
15	Biological crises (puberty, change of life, pregnancy)														②	1	②	②		
16	Loneliness																2	②	②	
17	Isolation, Imprisonment																	2	2	
18	Previous suicide attempts																		②	
19	Suicidal threats/suicidal thoughts																			
20	Death phantasies, death dreams																			
21	Suicides in family or close by																			
22	Anxiety																			
23	Blocking of aggression																			
24	Persistent insomnia																			
25	Alcohol abuse																			
26	Misuse of medicaments																			
27	Exogenous depression																			
28	Endogenous depression																			
29	Psychopathic personality																			
30	Neurotic disorders																			
31	Chronic alcoholism																			
32	Toxicomania (drug addiction)																			
33	Schizophrenia																			
34	Organic brain disease																			
35	Mental deficiency (oligophreny)																			

OF SUICIDALITY

20	21	22	㉓	24	㉕	26	27	28	㉙	30	31	32	33	34	35	
2	1	1	1	1	2	1	1	2	1	1	2	1	1	0	0	
2	1	①	1	①	1	2	2	②	1	1	1	2	1	0	0	18
2	1	1	1	1	1	1	2	1	1	1	1	1	1	0	0	
2	1	①	1	②	1	1	1	②	1	1	1	1	1	0	0	16
2	1	1	1	1	1	1	1	2	2	1	1	1	1	0	0	
2	1	①	1	①	1	1	2	②	1	1	1	1	1	0	0	15
2	1	1	1	1	1	1	2	2	1	1	1	1	1	0	0	
2	1	1	1	1	1	1	2	2	1	1	1	1	1	0	0	
1	1	⓪	0	⓪	1	0	0	⓪	0	0	0	0	0	0	0	9
2	1	⓪	1	①	1	1	2	①	2	2	2	1	2	1	1	14
2	1	①	1	①	1	1	2	①	2	2	1	2	1	0	1	13
2	1	1	1	1	2	2	2	1	2	2	2	2	2	2	2	
2	1	①	1	①	2	2	2	②	2	1	2	2	0	0	0	10
2	1	2	0	2	1	1	0	2	1	1	2	2	0	1	1	
2	1	②	1	②	2	2	2	②	1	1	1	1	1	0	1	12
2	1	②	2	②	2	1	2	②	2	2	2	2	1	2	1	10
2	1	2	2	2	0	0	0	0	2	0	2	2	0	0	1	
2	2	②	2	②	1	1	2	②	2	2	2	2	2	2	2	8
2	2	②	2	②	2	2	2	②	2	2	2	2	2	2	2	6
	2	2	2	2	2	2	2	2	2	2	2	2	2	2	2	
		0	0	0	0	2	2	2	2	0	0	0	0	0	0	
				2	②	2	1	2	②	2	2	2	2	2	2	4
					2	2	1	1	1	2	2	2	2	1	2	
						1	1	2	②	2	2	1	2	1	1	2
						2	2	1	2	1		2	1	2	2	
							2	1	2	1	2		0	1	1	
							2	2	2	2	2	2	2	2	2	
									2	2	2	2	2	2	2	
									2	2	2	2	2	2	2	
										2	2	2	2	2	2	
												2	2	2	2	
												1	2	1		
														1	1	
															1	

137

(Adapted from Pöldinger)

REFERENCE NOTES

Introduction

1. Pliny the Younger, *Letters* (Baltimore, Penguin Books), I, 2.

2. Richard H. Seiden, "Suicide among Youth, A Review of Literature 1900-67." Supplement to the *Bulletin of Suicidology*, December 1969.

3. José Ortega y Gasset, *The Revolt of the Masses* (New York: W. W. Norton, 1932).

4. Norman L. Farberow, *Bibliography on Suicide and Suicide Prevention* (Washington, D.C.: National Clearing House for Public Health Information, 1969); Hans Rost, *Bibliographie des Selbstmordes* (Augsburg, 1927); Norman L. Farberow and Edwin S. Shneidman, eds., *The Cry for Help* (New York: McGraw-Hill, 1961).

5. M. J. Kahne, "Suicide Research," *International Journal of Social Psychiatry* 12:177-186, 1966.

6. David Lester, "Suicidal Behavior, A Summary of Research Findings." (Mimeographed. Buffalo, N.Y.: Suicide Prevention and Crisis Service, 1970.)

7. Louis I. Dublin and B. Bunzel, *To Be or Not to Be* (New York: Smith & Haas, 1933).

1. Suicide in Retrospect

1. Voltaire, "Of Suicide," in *Works*, translated by T. Smollett, 4th ed. (Dublin, 1772), vol. XVII, pp. 165 ff.

2. Alfred Vierkandt, *Naturvölker und Kulturvölker* (Leipzig: Duncker and Humblot, 1896).

3. Edward Westermark, *The Origin and Development of the Moral Ideas* (London: Macmillan, 1906).

4. Halmuth H. Schaefer, "Can a Mouse Commit Suicide?" in E. S. Shneidman, ed., *Essays in Self-Destruction* (New York: Science House, 1967), pp. 494-509.

5. James Pritchard, ed., *Ancient Near Eastern Texts* (Princeton, N.J.: Princeton University Press, 1950), p. 405, ff.

6. Flavius Josephus, *The Jewish War*, translated by R. Trail (London, 1851), book 3, chapter 8; for selections from this work, see N. N. Glatzer, *Jerusalem and Rome* (New York: Meridian Books, 1960), pp. 283-290.

7. H. Romilly Fedden, *Suicide, a Social and Historical Study* (London: Peter Davies, 1938).

8. Herodotus, *Histories* (Baltimore: Penguin Books), p. 24.

9. *Ibid.*, p. 433.

10. Cicero, *Tusculanae Disputationes* [Tusculan Disputations], I, XXXIV, 83.

11. Helen Silving, "Suicide and Law," in Norman L. Farberow and Edwin Shneidman, eds., *Clues to Suicide* (New York: McGraw-Hill, 1957).

12. St. Augustine, *The City of God*, I, chapters XVI, XVII, XX, XXI, XXV.

13. St. Thomas Aquinas, *Summa Theologica*, II, ii, question 64, 5.

14. Pico della Mirandola, "Oration on the Dignity of Man," translated by Elizabeth L. Forbes, in Ernst Cassirer, Paul O. Kristeller, and John H. Randall, Jr., eds., *The Renaissance Philosophy of Man* (Chicago: University of Chicago Press, 1948), pp. 223-254.

15. In Hoyt H. Hudson's translation (Princeton, N. J.: Princeton University Press, 1941, paperback, 1970), p. 41, this is rendered as "people who live next door to wisdom."

16. Sir Thomas More, *Utopia*, book 2.

17. Robert Burton, *The Anatomy of Melancholy* (London: Chatto & Windus, 1907, p. 288.

18. Johann Robeck, *Exercitatio philosophia de morte voluntaria* (Rintelli, 1736).

19. Charles Moore, *A Full Inquiry into the Subject of Suicide,* (London, 1790).

Reference Notes

20. Madame de Staël, *Reflexions sur le suicide* (London, 1813).
21. Fedden, *op. cit.*, p. 283.
22. Léon Meynard, *Le Suicide, étude morale et métaphysique*, (Paris: P.U.F., 1966), p. 105.
23. *Ibid.*, p. 111.
24. *Ibid.*, p. 116.

2. Facts and Figures

1. U.S. Bureau of Census, *Statistical Abstract of the United States*, 89th ed. (Washington, D.C., 1968).
2. *World Health Statistics Annuals* (Geneva: World Health Organization), vol. 21, no. 6, 1968.
3. See Jacques Choron, "Suicide in Soviet Russia," *Bulletin of Suicidology*, December 1968.
4. J. T. Massey, *Suicide in the United States*, (PHS Publication 1000, series 20, no. 5, Washington, D.C.: U.S. Department of Health, Education, and Welfare, 1967).
5. Werner Simon and G. K. Lumry, "Suicide among Physician-Patients," *Journal of Nervous and Mental Disease*, vol. 147, no. 2, 1968; W. Freeman, "Psychiatrists Who Kill Themselves," paper presented at American Psychiatric Association meeting, Detroit, May 1967.

3. Methods of Suicide

1. John Webster, *The Duchess of Malfi* (ca. 1614).
2. H. J. Bochnik, *Verzweiflung* [Despair] (Stuttgart, Enke, 1962), pp. 201 ff.
3. Romi, *Suicides* (Paris: Editions Serg, 1964), is the source for this case, as well as for most of the other bizarre suicides cited in the preceding paragraphs.

4. Attempted Suicide

1. Edwin S. Shneidman and Norman L. Farberow, "Statistical Comparison between Attempted and Committed Suicides" in Norman L. Farberow and Edwin S. Shneidman, eds., *The Cry for Help* (New York: McGraw-Hill, 1961), pp. 19-48.

2. D. Parkin and Erwin Stengel, "Incidence of Suicidal Attempts in an Urban Community," *British Medical Journal* 2:133, 1965.

3. H. Jacobziner, "Attempted Suicides in Adolescence," *Journal of the American Medical Association:* 191-7-11, 1965.

4. Shneidman and Farberow, "Statistical Comparison ...," p. 46.

5. Parkin and Stengel, *op. cit.*

6. Erwin Stengel, *Suicide and Attempted Suicide* (Baltimore: Penguin Books, Pelican Original, 1964), p. 72.

7. Shneidman and Farberow, "Statistical Comparison ...," p. 19.

8. *Ibid.*

9. J. E. Lennard-Jones and Robert Asher, "Why Do They Do It?," *Lancet*, 1, 1959, p. 1138.

10. Neil Kessel and Wallace McCulloch, "Repeated Acts of Self-poisoning and Self-injury," *Proceedings of the Royal Society of Medicine*, 59 (2):89-92, 1966.

11. Nilima Chowdhury and Norman Kreitman, "A Comparison of Parasuicides ('Attempted Suicide') and the Clients of the Telephone Samaritan Service," *Applied Social Studies*, vol. 3, 1971, pp. 51-57.

12. Ronald S. Mintz, "Prevalence of Persons in the City of Los Angeles Who Have Attempted Suicide," *Bulletin of Suicidology*, Fall 1970.

13. W. Heimerzheim, "Uber den Selbstmord bei nicht-psychotischen Persoenlichkeiten" [On Suicide among Non-psychotic Personalities], Medical dissertation, Cologne, 1933,

14. K. Ohara, S. Aizawa, and S. Shimizu, [A Clinical Study of Double Love Suicide], in Japanese, *Journal of Japanese Medicine*, August 1962, pp. 34-47.

15. E. C. Trautman, "The Suicidal Fit," *Journal of Psychiatry*, 119:228, 1961.

Reference Notes

5. Suicide among Adolescents

1. A. MacDonald, "Statistics of Child Suicide," *American Statistical Association Publication* 10:260-264, 1906-1907.

2. D. Mulcock, "Juvenile Suicide, A Study of Suicide and Attempted Suicide over a 16-Year Period," *Medical Officer* 94:155-160, 1955.

3. Richard H. Seiden, "Suicide Among Youth, A Review of the Literature, 1900-1967." Supplement, *Bulletin of Suicidology*, December 1969.

4. *Ibid.*, table 3, p. 5.

5. *Ibid.*, table 9, p. 21.

6. Michael L. Peck and Sam M. Heilig.

7. André Haim, *Le Suicide d'Adolescents*, (Paris: Payot, 1969), pp. 187-192.

8. *Ibid.*, pp. 246, 253.

9. *Ibid.*, p. 294.

6. The Search for Causes

1. Curt Michael, ed., *Abschied* [Farewell] (Zurich: Oprecht, 1947).

2. *Ibid.*

3. Walter Pöldinger, "Vereinsamung und Selbstmord" [Loneliness and Suicide], *Wiener Medizinsche Wochenschrift* 12:225-231, 1969.

4. Robert Gaupp, "Uber den Selbstmord" [On Suicide], *Arztliche Rundschau*, 1910.

5. Pöldinger, *op. cit.*

6. Erwin Ringel, *Der Selbstmord, Abschluss einer krankhaften psychischen Entwicklung* [Suicide, End Result of a Pathological Psychical Development] (Vienna-Dusseldorf: Maudrich, 1953).

7. Jean Etienne Dominique Esquirol, *Des maladies mentales considerés sous les rapports medicals, hygieniques et medico-legals* (Paris, 1838), vol. I, p. 639; English translation by E. K. Hunt, entitled *Mental Maladies: Treatise on Insanity* (Philadelphia, 1845).

8. Esquirol, *op. cit.*, vol. I, p. 655.
9. A. F. Brierre de Boismont, *Du suicide et de la folie suicide* [On Suicide and Suicidal Insanity] (Paris, 1856; 2nd ed. 1965), p. 331.
10. Esquirol, *op. cit.*, vol. I, p. 655.
11. H. W. Gruhle, *Selbstmord* [Suicide] (Leipzig: Thieme, 1940).
12. Auguste Comte, *Le philosophie positive,* edited by Emile Rigolage (Paris: Flammarian, 1910), vol. III, p. 292.
13. Jack D. Douglas, *The Social Meanings of Suicide* (Princeton, N.J.: Princeton University Press, 1967), p. 18.
14. Maurice Halbwachs, *Les Causes du suicide* (Paris: Alcan, 1930), p. 30.
15. Paul Friedman, ed., *On Suicide* (New York: International University Press, 1967); English translation of the Minutes of the 1910 meeting of the Vienna Psychoanalytic Society, with a brief introduction by the editor.
16. Robert Litman, "Sigmund Freud on Suicide," in Edwin S. Shneidman, ed., *Essays in Self-Destruction* (New York: Science House, 1967).
17. Sigmund Freud, *An Outline of Psychoanalysis,* Standard Edition of the Complete Psychological Works (London: Hogarth Press, 1953-1965), vol. 23, pp. 148-150.
18. Karl Menninger, *Man Against Himself* (New York: Harcourt Brace, 1938), p. 50.
19. *Ibid.*, p. 68.
20. *Ibid.*, p. 73.
21. For details about the origins and criticism of the death-instinct hypothesis, see Jacques Choron, *Modern Man and Mortality* (New York: Macmillan, 1964).
22. Quoted in "Suicide," *Great Medical Encyclopedia* (Moscow, 1963), vol. 29 (in Russian).

7. Suicide and Mental Disorders

1. *Prevention of Suicide,* Public Health Paper No. 35 (Geneva: World Health Organization, 1968), p. 61.

Reference Notes

2. Erwin Stengel, "Classification of Mental Disorders," *Bulletin of the World Health Organization* 21:601-663, 1960.

3. Alex D. Pokorny, "Suicide Rates in Various Psychiatric Disorders," *Journal of Nervous and Mental Disease* 139:499-506,1964.

4. F. N. Pitts, Jr., and G. Winokur, "Affective Disorders, III: Diagnostic Correlates and Incidence of Suicide," *Journal of Nervous and Mental Disease* 139(2):176-181,1964.

5. Aaron T. Beck, *Depression* (New York: Harper & Row, 1967), pp. 60-65.

6. Paul Kielholz, *Diagnose und Therapie der Depressionen für den Praktiker* (Munich: Lehmanns Verlag, 1966), pp. 83-95; Paul Kielholz and Walter Pöldinger, "Antidepressive Drug Therapy in Clinic and Practice," *Clinical Psychopharmacology* 1:73-87, 1968.

7. Beck, *op. cit.*, p. 307.

8. For a discussion of the possible impact of the ideas about death held by an individual on his suicidal behavior (suicide-promoting or suicide-inhibiting), see Jacques Choron, "Suicide and the Notions of Death," *Proceedings of the Fourth International Conference for Suicide Prevention*, 1967 (Los Angeles: Delmar Publishing Co., 1968), pp. 268-277. For a large-scale investigation of 200 patients in Germany directly after their frustrated suicide attempts, see Gerhard Irle, "Einstellung zum Tod bei Patienten nach Selbstmordversuch," [Attitude toward Death in Patients after a Suicide Attempt] *Der Nervenarzt* 39:255-260, 1968.

9. Charles Zwingmann, *Zur Psychologie der Lebenskrisen* [On the Psychology of Life Crises], (Frankfurt am Main: Akademische Verlagsgesellschaft, 1962), Introduction.

10. Sir Thomas Browne, *Religio Medici.*

8. Suicide Prevention

1. For information on issues involved in setting up and staffing suicide prevention (and "crisis intervention") centers, and on treatment of suicidal individuals, see H. L. R. Resnick, ed., *Suicidal Behaviors, Diagnosis and Management* (Boston: Little, Brown, 1968), particularly Ronald S. Mintz, "The Psychotherapy of the Suicidal Patient," pp. 271-296.

2. James Hillman, *Suicide and the Soul* (New York, Harper & Row, 1964).

3. Christopher Bagley, "The Evaluation of Effectiveness of a Suicide Prevention Scheme by an Ecological Method," *Social Science and Medicine* (London) 2: 1-14, 1968.

4. *Bulletin of Suicidology* 6:17, 1970.

5. *Ibid.*, p. 25.

6. Erwin Stengel, *Suicide and Attempted Suicide*, (Baltimore: Penguin Books, 1964), p. 128.

9. The Psychological Autopsy

1. These cases are taken from Theodore J. Curphey, M.D., "The Psychological Autopsy," *Bulletin of Suicidology*, July 1968.

2. Theodore C. Curphey, in "The Question of Suicide," *Roche Medical Image and Commentary* (New York: International Medical Press, 1969), p. 28.

3. A. W. Stearns, "Cases of Probable Suicide in Young Persons without Obvious Motivation," *Journal of the Maine Medical Association* 44: 16-22, 1953; L. W. Shankel and A. C. Carr, "Transvestism and Hanging in a Male Adolescent," *Psychiatric Quarterly* 30: 478-493, 1956.

10. Terms and Definitions

1. Edward Phillips, *New World of Words* (1662).

2. Immanuel Kant, *Metaphysik der Sitten* [Metaphysics of Morals] (1797), Part II.

3. G. Deshaies, *Psychologie du Suicide* (Paris: P.U.F., 1947), p. 5; "*acte de se tuer d'une manière habituellement consciente, en prenant la mort comme moyen ou comme fin.*"

4. Emile Durkheim, *Le Suicide*, new ed. (Paris: P.U.F., 1960), p. 246. "*Pour qu'il y ait suicide, il suffit que l'acte d'ou la mort doit nécessairement resulter, ait été accompli par la victime en connaissance de cause.*"

Reference Notes

5. Emile Durkheim, *Suicide* (New York: The Free Press, 1951), p. 45-46.

11. *The Problem of "Rational Suicide"*

1. Fred Dubitscher, Wolfgang De Boor, A. Langelüdecke, among others.
2. Charles Neuringer, "Rigid Thinking in Suicidal Individuals," *Journal of Consulting Psychology* 28: 54-58, 1964.
3. Edwin S. Shneidman and Norman L. Farberow, eds., *Clues to Suicide* (New York: McGraw-Hill, 1957).
4. Pliny the Younger, *Letters* (Baltimore, Penguin Books), I, 12.
5. *Ibid.*, I, 23.
6. Paul Pretzel, "Philosophical and Ethical Considerations of Suicide Prevention," *Bulletin of Suicidology*, July 1968, p. 30.

12. *The Problem of "Easy Dying"*

1. Blaise Pascal, "Vie de Blaise Pascal" in Blaise Pascal, *Pensees et Opuscules*. 12th ed. (Paris: Hachette), p. 37.
2. Seneca, Letter to Lucilius, no. 70, in *The Stoic Philosophy of Seneca*, translated by Moses Hadas (Garden City, N.Y.: Doubleday Anchor Books, 1958), pp. 202 ff.
3. Friedrich Nietzche, *Human All-Too-Human (Menschliches Allzumenschliches*, 1877-78; Stuttgart: Kröner Verlag, 1954), Vol. I, aphorism 80.
4. For an attempt at an explanation of this phenomenon, see Herbert Hendin, *Suicide and Scandinavia* (New York, Grune and Stratton, 1964).
5. Strabo, *Geography*, X, 4860.
6. Aelian (Claudius Aelianus), *Varia Historia*, III, 37.
7. Norman L. Farberow, Edwin S. Shneidman, and C. Leonard, *Suicide among General Medical and Surgical Hospital Patients with Malignant Neoplasms* (Washington, D.C.: Veterans Administration, 1963).

13. Philosophers on Suicide

1. Plato, *Phaedo*, 62 b, translated by Benjamin Jowett (in Plato, *Republic and Other Works*, New York: Doubleday, Dolphin Books).
2. *Ibid.*, 64 c.
3. *Ibid.*, 64 a.
4. *Ibid.*, 63 c.
5. Plato, *The Laws*, 873, translated by A. E. Taylor (London: J. M. Dent & Sons, 1934).
6. Aristotle, *Nicomachean Ethics*, translated by W. D. Ross, 1115 a, 25, and 1116, 10.
7. *Ibid.*, 1138 a, 5.
8. H. Usener, ed., *Epicurea*, Fragment 221 (Leipzig, 1887); English translation in Whitney J. Oates, *The Stoic and the Epicurean Philosophers*, (New York: Random House, 1940), p. 31 (the Epicurus fragments are translated by C. Bailey).
9. Oates, *op. cit.*, Epicurus, Letter to Menoeceus, p. 31.
10. *Ibid.*, p. 43.
11. *Ibid.*, p. 31.
12. *Ibid.*
13. Lucretius, *On the Nature of the Universe*, translation by Ronald Latham (Baltimore: Penguin Books, 1951), book III, 61.
14. *Ibid.*, book III, 916.
15. Cicero, *De Finibus Bonorum et Malorum* (45 B.C.), VII, 28, 176.
16. Seneca, Letter to Lucilius, no. 70, in *The Stoic Philosophy of Seneca*, translated by Moses Hadas, (Garden City, N.Y.: Doubleday Anchor Books), pp. 202 ff.
17. Oates, *op. cit.*, Epictetus, *Discourses*, translated by P. E. Matheson, book I, chapter IX.
18. *Ibid.*, book I, chapter XXIV, 9.
19. Michel de Montaigne, *Essais*, edited by Albert Thibaudet, Bibliothèque de la Pléiade (Paris: Nouvelle Revue Française, 1946), book II, chapter 3.

Reference Notes

20. René Descartes, *Oeuvres et Lettres*, Bibliothèque de la Pléiade (Paris: Gallimard, 1963), p. 1219.

21. *Ibid.*, p. 1220.

22. *Ibid.*, p. 1225.

23. Benedict de Spinoza, *Ethics*, IV, note to Proposition XX, in *The Chief Works of Benedict de Spinoza*, translated by R. H. M. Elwes (New York: Dover Press, 1951), vol. II, p. 203.

24. *Ibid.*

25. Baron Paul Henri Dietrich d'Holbach, *Système de la nature, ou les lois du monde physique et du monde moral* (1770); English translation *The System of Nature; or The Laws of the Moral and Physical World* (London, 1795); first American edition (New York, 1835).

26. Voltaire, "Of Suicide," in *Works*, translated by T. Smollett. 4th ed. (Dublin, 1772), vol. XVII, pp. 165 ff.

27. Montesquieu, *Persian Letters*, nos. 76 and 77, in *Complete Works*, (London, 1777), vol. III.

28. Denis Diderot *et al.*, *Encyclopédie* (Classiques Larousse series).

29. Jean-Jacques Rousseau, *La Nouvelle Héloise* (Larousse).

30. David Hume, "On Suicide," *Essays, Moral, Political and Literary*, new ed. (New York: Oxford University Press, 1963), p. 590.

31. Immanuel Kant, *Metaphysik der Sitten* (Metaphysics of Morals) (1797), Part II.

32. Arthur Schopenhauer, *The World as Will and Idea*, translated by T. B. Haldane and J. Kemp (London: Routledge & Kegan Paul, 1883), vol. I, p. 362.

33. *Ibid.*, vol. I, p. 515.

34. *Ibid.*

35. *Ibid.*, *Parerga und Paralipomena*, 2nd part, chapter XIII, in Collected Works, 5 vols. (Leipzig: Inselverlag), vol. V, p. 332 ff.

36. Giacomo Leopardi, *Essays, Dialogues and Thoughts*, translated by James Thomson (New York, 1905).

37. "The Life of Plotinus by Porphyry," in Plotinus, *The Enneads*, vol. I.

38. Friedrich Nietzsche, "Letter to Malwida Meysenburg" January 14, 1880, in *Gesammelte Briefe* [Collected Letters], Elizabeth Förster–

SUICIDE

Nietzsche, Peter Gast, *et al.*, eds., 5 vols. (Leipzig, 1900-1909); the same thought is expressed in *Die Unschuld des Werdens — Aus dem Nachlass* [The Innocence of Becoming — Posthumous Writings] (Stuttgart: Kröner Verlag, 1956), vol. I, p. 254

39. Nietzsche, *Beyond Good and Evil (Jenseits von Gut und Böse*, 1886; Stuttgart: Kröner Verlag, 1953), aphorism 157, p. 89.

40. Nietzsche, *The Dawn of Day (Morgenröte*, 1881; Stuttgart: Kröner Verlag, 1953), p. 210.

41. Nietzsche, *Human All-Too-Human (Menschliches Allzumenschliches*, 1877-78; Stuttgart: Kröner Verlag, 1954), aphorism 88.

42. Nietzsche, *Thus Spake Zarathustra (Also Sprach Zarathustra*, 1883; Stuttgart: Kröner Verlag, 1956), part I, p. 76.

43. Nietzsche, *The Will to Power (Der Wille zur Macht*, 1888; Stuttgart: Kröner Verlag, 1952), p. 697.

44. Eduard von Hartmann, *Zur Geschichte und Begründung des Pessimismus* [History and Justification of Pessimism] (Berlin: Carl Dunker, 1880).

45. Eduard von Hartmann, *Ethische Studien* [Ethical Studies] (Leipzig: Hermann Haacke, 1898), p. 189.

46. Albert Camus, *The Myth of Sisyphus*, translated by Justin O'Brien (New York: Alfred A. Knopf, Vintage Books, 1955), p. 7.

47. *Ibid.*, p. 40.

48. *Ibid.*, p. 43.

49. Philip Thody, *Albert Camus* (New York: Grove Press, 1957), p. 12.

14. Suicide and the Meaning of Life

1. Margarete von Andics, *Suicide and the Meaning of Life* (London: Hodge & Co., 1947), page 9; first published in German as *Sinn und Sinnlosigkeit des Lebens* [The Meaning and Meaninglessness of Life] (Vienna: Gerold & Co., 1938).

2. *Ibid.*, p. 33.

3. *Ibid.*, p. 196.

4. *Ibid.*, p. 181.

Reference Notes

5. Paul Edwards, "Life, the Meaning and Value of," *Encyclopedia of Philosophy*, Paul Edwards, general editor (New York: Macmillan, 1967).

6. See Jacques Choron, *Modern Man and Mortality* (New York: Macmillan, 1964), pp. 167-171.

7. Albert Camus, *The Myth of Sisyphus* (New York: Alfred A. Knopf, Vintage Books, 1955), p. 7.

8. William James, *The Will to Believe* (New York: Longmans Green 1897), pp. 37-62.

9. Georg Siegmund, *Sein oder Nichtsein, die Frage des Selbstmordes* [To Be or Not to Be, the Problem of Suicide] (Trier: Paulinus Verlag, 1961).

10. Georg Siegmund, *Gott* (Bern: Franke, 1963), p. 10-12.

11. Erwin Ringel, "Das Werterleben der Selbstmoerder" [The Value-Experience of Suicides], *Der Selbstmord, Beitrage zur Neurologie und Psychiatrie*, 3: 154-171, 1953.

12. Erwin Ringel, "Uber Selbtsmordversuche von Jugendlichen" [On Suicide Attempts of Juveniles], *Internationale Journal für Prophylactische Medizin und Socialhygiene* 2: 39-44, 1959.

13. Victor Frankl, *Ärztliche Seelsorge* [Medical-Pastoral Counseling] (Vienna: Deuticke, 1952), p. 48.

14. Presumably Ringel is referring to *The Will to Power*, Book 3, Section 3: "When one is clear in one's own mind about the 'why' of his life, one easily disregards its 'how'."

15. Ringel, "Uber Selbstmordversuche von Jugendlichen," *op. cit.*

16. Schultz-Hencke, *Der Gehemmte Mensch* [The Handicapped Man] (Leipzig: Thieme, 1940).

17. Ernest Jones, *The Life and Work of Sigmund Freud* (New York: Basic Books, 1957), vol. III, p. 465. Jones reproduces the letter in English but it is clear that it was written either in French (which Freud knew very well) or in German. The latter is more probable since the letter begins "Meine liebe Marie." If such is indeed the case, then what Jones renders as "sense or value of life" must be the German *Sinn und Wert des Lebens*, and *Sinn* is more correctly translated as "meaning" than as "sense."

18. Carl Jung, "Seele und Tod" [The Soul and Death], in *Die Wirklichkeit der Seele* [The Reality of the Soul] (Zurich: Rascher, 1939).

19. Victor Frankl, *From Death Camp to Existentialism* (Boston: Beacon Press, 1959), p. 101.

20. Adam Schaff, *A Philosophy of Man* (New York: Monthly Review Press, 1962), pp. 35, 53.

Conclusion

1. U.S. Bureau of the Census, *Statistical Abstracts of the United States, 1968.*

2. *The Facts of Life and Death,* Public Health Publication No. 600, Selected Statistics, U.S. Department of Health, Education and Welfare, Washington, D.C., 1965.

3. Pliny the Elder, *Historia naturalis* (Loeb Classical Library), book 2, VI, 28, "... *ne deum quidem posse omnia. Namque nec sibi potest mortem concicere, si velit, quod homini dedi optimum in tantis vitae poenis.*"

INDEX

accidental suicide, 88, 89, 90
accidents, "purposeful," 34, 71
Acosta, Uriel, 58-59, 60
Adler, Alfred, 68, 140
adolescents, suicide of, 51-55, 60
"advocate of death," see Hegesias
afterlife, expectation of, 13, 21
age, suicide rate according to, 37
aggressive instincts, 69
Albigensian doctrine, 25, 27
alcohol addiction, 71, 94
Alembert, Jean d', 126
altruistic suicide, 66, 67
Andics, Margarete von, 139-141
animals, 11
anomic suicide, 66, 67
"anomie," 66, 67
antidepressants, 77
antiquity, 12-22
Aquinas, Saint Thomas, 25, 123
apology for suicide, 27, 30, 31
Aristotle, 77, 110-112
Arria, suicide of, 23
asceticism, 71
Asher, R., 48
attempted suicide:
 definitions, 43-46
 in mental disorders, 75
 statistical estimates, 49

attitudes toward suicide, 3, 5, 7
Augustine, Saint, 25, 123
Austria, suicide figures, 35

Bagley, Christopher, 82
balance-sheet suicides *(Bilanz-Selbstmord)*, 96-97
Balzac, Honoré, 31
Beyond the Pleasure Principle (Sigmund Freud), 70
"*biaiothanatoi*," 3
bibliographies on suicide, 6
Biothanatos (John Donne), 28
bizarre suicides, 41-42
"Black Death," 26
Bochnik, H.J., 39
Boismont, see Brierre de Boismont
Bourdin, Claude Etienne, 5
Brierre de Boismont, A. F., 61, 63
"broken home," 84-85
Browne, Sir Thomas, 78
Buddha, Siddartha Gautama, 19
Burton, Robert *(Anatomy of Melancholy)*, 5, 28

Camus, Albert *(The Myth of Sisyphus)*, 136-138, 142, 144
Canada, suicide figures, 35

canine behavior, 11
Cardano, Gerolamo, 38
Carthage, 24
Catholicism, 25
causes of suicide, the problem of, 61-73, 154-155
Center for the Study of Suicide Prevention, 80
Chateaubriand, François René, 31
Christianity, 21, 24, 25, 26, 32, 58
"chronic" suicide, 71
Cicero, 20, 22
civic duty, 22
classification of suicides:
    Durkheim, 66
    Meninnger, 71
Cleanthes, 115
"clinical" depression, 75, 76
Cohen, Sidney, 54
"collective consciousness," 65
comparative statistics on suicide, 35
Comte, Auguste, 64-65
"conatus" (Spinoza), 123-124
Corcyra, mass suicides at, 17
"cries for help," 4, 7, 46, 47
"criminal" aspect of suicide, 128
Curphey, Theodore C., 88
Cynics, 112
Cyrenaics, 112

dangerous sports, 47
Darwin, Charles, 66
death:
    "complete" discovery of, 10
    fear of, 78
    Orphic conception of, 18
death instinct *(Todestrieb)*, 70-71
deaths from all causes compared to suicide rate, 154
definitions of suicide, 91-95
"deliberate self-injury," 48
"deliberate self-poisoning," 48
Democritus, 18, 115
Denmark, 35, 104

depression, 77, 126
depressive illness, 76, 77
Descartes, René, 120-122
Desfontaines, Abbé, 92
Deshaies, G., 80, 93
destructive instinct, 69
"Dialogue of a Misanthrope with His Own Soul" ("Dispute over Suicide") (ancient Egyptian text), 12
Diderot, Denis, 125-126
domestic gas, suicide by, 38
Donne, John *(Biothanatos)*, 28
Dostoevski, Fëdor; 31; *Diary of a Writer*, 51
Douglas, Jack D., 67
drowning, suicide by, 39
drug deaths, 88
drugs, 54, 71
Dublin, Louis *(To Be or Not to Be)*, 7
Dumas, Jean, 5
Durkheim, Emile, 6, 65, 67, 68, 80, 93-94

"easy dying," 102-106
Edwards, Paul, 141-142
egoistic suicide, 66, 67
Egyptians, ancient, 12
eighteenth-century attitudes, 28-30
eighteenth-century philosophers, 124
"embryonic" suicide, 94
Encyclopedists, 126
"endura" (suicide by voluntary fasting), 26
England and Wales, suicide figures, 35, 52
Epictetus, 116, 117
Epicurus, 112-115
Erasmus, 26
Esprit des lois, De l' (Montesquieu), 92
Esquirol, Jean E. D., 5, 61, 63
Euripedes, 18
euthanasia, 102-104

Index

"euthanatic" suicide, 105
evaluation of suicidal risk, 159-161
"existential emptiness," 147

Farberow, Norman L., 6, 43, 48, 80, 97
"Fatalist, The" (Mikhail Lermontov), 47
Fedden, H. Romilly, 18, 31-32
firearms and explosives, suicide by, 38, 39, 41
France, suicide figures, 35
Frankl, Victor, 147, 149
Freud, Sigmund, 68, 69, 70, 123, 148-149

Galen, 5
gas, suicide by, 38
Gaupp, Robert, 62
German Federal Republic, suicide figures, 35
Goethe, Johann Wolfgang von *(The Sorrows of Young Werther)*, 31
"goal-reflex" theory, 72-72
Greece, suicide figures, 35
Greeks, ancient, 15
Gruhle, H. W., 64, 80

Haiduk, Julius, 60
Haim, André, 54, 55
Halbwachs, Maurice, 68
hanging, suicide by, 38-39
hara-kiri, 66, 93, 97
Hartmann, Eduard von, 135-136
Hebrews, ancient, 13, 14
Hegesias, 20
Heimerzheim, W., 50
hemlock, 19, 20, 21, 105
heroic suicides, 22-23
Herodotus, 18, 19
Hillman, James *(Suicide and the Soul)*, 82
Hippocrates, 5
Hoche, Alfred, 96
Holbach, Paul H. D. d', 124
Homer, 15

homicide, 10
Horace, 22
Human All-Too-Human (Nietzsche), 134
Hume, David ("On Suicide"), 29-30, 127
Hungary, suicide figures, 35

Iliad, 18
immolation, 27
immortality, belief in, 13, 107, 109
instincts, basic, 69-70
interpersonal conflicts, 162
"Is Life Worth Living?" (William James), 143-145
isolation, 12
Italy, suicide figures, 35

Jacobziner, H., 43
James, William ("Is Life Worth Living?"), 143-145
Japan, suicide figures, 35, 52
Jerome, Saint, 114
Jews, early, 26
Job, 13
Josephus, Flavius, 14-15
Jung, Carl, 149
juveniles, 53-55

Kahne, M. J., 7
Kammerer, Paul, 59
Kant, Immanuel, 91, 129-130
Keats, John, 31
Keos (Kea), Isle of, 105, 119, 120
Kessel, Neil, 48
Kielholz, Paul, 81, 158
Kierkegaard, Søren, 32
Kreitman, Norman, 48
"Krisentoleranz" (capacity to endure a crisis) (Charles Swingmann), 78

Lafargue, Paul, 100-101
Lamartine, Alphonse de, 31
last messages, 57-61
Laws, The (Plato), 110

Leibnitz, Gottfried Wilhelm von, 135
lemmings, 11
Lennard-Jones, J. E., 48
Leopardi, Giacomo, 132-133
Lermontov, Mikhail, 31, 47
Lester, David, 7
"Letters to Lucilius" (Seneca), 116-117
Lettres Persanes (Montesquieu), 125
life and death, attitudes toward, 4-5
List, Friedrich, 57, 61
Litman, Robert E., 69, 80, 83
loneliness, 12, 13, 62, 140
Los Angeles Suicide Prevention Center, 53, 80, 87
Lucretia, 23-24, 25
Lucretius *(De Rerum Natura)*, 114-115
LSD, 54

MacDonald, A., 51
Madagascar, mass suicides on, 9
marital status in relation to suicide, 36, 54
Mark Antony, 20-21
martyrdom, 71
Marxism, 150
Masaryk, Thomas, 6
masochistic mutilation, 46
mass suicides, 9, 17, 27
Massada fortress, 14
meaning of life, 137, 139-151
melancholia, 5
Memoire sur le suicide (Merian), 30
men, compared with women, 36, 39, 44, 45
Menninger, Karl, 70, 71, 80, 94
mental illness, 5, 63, 72, 73, 74-78
methods of suicide, 38-42
Meynard, Léon, 32, 33
Middle Ages, 24-26
Mintz, Ronald S., 49, 169
misconceptions ("myths") about suicide, 81

Monroe, Marilyn, 88
Montaigne, 118-120
Montesquieu, 92, 125
Moore, Charles *(A Full Inquiry into the Subject of Suicide)*, 30
More, Thomas *(Utopia)*, 26
Morselli, Enrico *(Il suicido)*, 6
Moslems, 26
motives for suicide, 10, 56, 62
Mulcock, D., 52
Myth of Sisyphus, The (Albert Camus), 137, 138, 142

Napoleon, 30-31
National Save-a-Life League, 79-80
Neo-Positivists, 149
Nero, 22, 23
Netherlands, suicide figures, 35
Neuringer, Charles, 97
neuroses, 75
New World of Words (Edward Phillips), 91
New Zealand, suicide figures, 9
Nietzsche, Friedrich Wilhelm, 104, 133-134
"non-whites," 37
Northern Ireland, suicide figures, 35
Norway, suicide figures, 35, 52
Novalis, 31

Odysseus, 15, 16, 17
Ohara, K. (with S. Aizawa and S. Shimizu), 50
old age, escape from, 99
Old Testament, suicides in, 13
"On Suicide" (David Hume), 29-30, 127-129
"On Suicide Attempts of Juveniles" (Erwin Ringel), 147-148
Oppenheim, David E., 68
Oretega y Gasset, José, 4

Panaetius, 116
"parasuicide," 48

Index

"partial" suicide, 71
Pascal, Blaise, 103
Paul, Jean, 31
Pavlov, Ivan, 72-73, 146
Peisithanatos, see Hegesias
personality types, unstable, 44
pessimism, 19, 130-132, 135-136
Petronius, 23
Pharisees, 14
pharmacotherapy, 77
Phillips, Edward *(New World of Words)*, 91
physical illness (terminal), 105-106
physicians, suicide rate among, 105
Pitts, F. N., Jr., 76
Plato:
    The Laws, 110
    Phaedo, 20, 22, 108-109
Pliny the Elder, 156
Pliny the Younger, 4, 23, 98-99
Plotinus and Porphyry, discussion of suicide, 133
poison, suicide by, 39
Pokorny, Alex D., 76
Poland, suicide figures, 35
Pöldinger, Walter, 62, 63, 81, 96, 158
Portugal, suicide figures, 35
Posidonius, 116
prevention of suicide, 79-85, 151, 155; see also suicide prevention
primitive cultures, 9-11
Protestantism, 25
"protosuicide," 48
"pseudocide," 48
psychiatrists, suicide rate among, 37
psychoanalysis, 68
psychodynamics of suicide, 46
psychological autopsy, 83, 86-90
psychological factors, 62
psychoses, 75
Ptolemy II, 20
Puerto Rican immigrants, 50

"purposeful" accidents, 71
Pythagoras, 128

Raskolniki (Russian sect), 26-27
rational suicide, 64, 96-101
religion, 33, 65, 67, 103, 151
Renaissance, 27-28
Ringel, Erwin, 63, 81, 146-148, 158
risk-taking activities, 71
Robeck, Johann, 28-29
Roland, Jean-Marie, 58
Romans, 20-24
Romantic Movement, 31
Rost, Hans, 6
Rousseau, Jean-Jacques, 9, 28, 58, 60, 61, 126-127
Rudolf, Archduke of Austria, 57, 61
Rufus, Corellius, 23, 99
Russian Orthodox Church, 26
Russian roulette, 47

Sadger, Isidor, 68
Samaritans, the, 80, 82
Sartre, Jean-Paul, 62
Schaefer, Halmuth, 11
Schaff, Adam, 150
Schneider, Pierre B., 45
school of suicide, 20
Schopenhauer, Arthur, 130-133
Scotus, Duns, 123
Seidel, Alfred, 146
Sein oder Nichtsein (To Be or Not to Be) (Georg Siegmund), 146
"self-damage," 44-45, 46
self-destructive tendencies, 71
Seneca, 22, 23, 93, 103, 116
Sevigné, Madame de, 41
sex differences, 44
Shakespeare's tragedies, suicides in, 27
Shelley, Percy Bysshe, 31
Shneidman, Edwin S., 43, 48, 69, 70, 80, 87
Siegmund, Georg *(Sein oder Nichtsein)*, 146

Silius Italicus, 23
Silving, Helen, 21
single persons, suicide among, 54
sleeping pills, 38, 41, 46
social isolation, 12
"social reality," 67
"social solidarity," 66
sociological factors, 62
Socrates, 20, 109
Solon, 18
Sophocles, 18
Soviet Union, suicide figures, 36
Spinoza, 60, 122-124
Staël, Madame de, 30
statistics of suicide, 5-6, 35, 49, 76, 83-84, 152-154
Stekel, Wilhelm, 68
Stengel, Erwin S., 43, 44, 49, 85, 105
Stoics, 20, 30, 113, 115-118, 129
Strabo, 105
suicide among primitives, 9
suicide contemplators, 84
suicide notes, 57-60, 86
suicide prevention:
    evaluation of effectiveness, 82-85
    history, 80
    objections to, 81-82
suttee, 66
Sweden, suicide figures, 35, 104
Switzerland, suicide figures, 35, 52

Tacitus, 21
taedium vitae, 21
Tagore, Rabindranath, 140
terminology, disagreements in, 61-62, 91-95
Thanatos, 102, 123
Theognis of Megara, 18, 19
therapy, electroconvulsive (ECT), 77
Thody, Philip, 138
Thomas, Klaus, 81
Thucydides, 17
Todestrieb, 70

Tolstoy, Leo *(Anna Karenina)*, 142-143
transmigration of the soul, doctrine of, 108
Trautman, E. C., 50

United States, suicide figures, 34-36, 52-53, 154-155

Valerius Maximus, 21
Valery, Paul, 62
"Value-Experience of Suicide" (Erwin Ringel), 146-147
Varah, Chad, 80
Vetsera, Baroness Mary, 57, 61
Vienna Psychoanalytical Society, 51, 68
Vierkandt, Alfred, 9
Voltaire, 9, 29, 92, 124-125
voluntary fasting ("endura"), 26, 39

Warren, Harry, 80
West Berlin, suicide figures, 25
Westermark, Edward, 10
West Germany, suicide figures, 52
Winokur, F., 76
witches, 26
wives of priests, 26
Wold, Carl, 83-84
women, 10, 23-24, 25, 43, 45
World Health Organization, suicide figures, 35

Xenophon, 19
Xerxes, 19

young persons, suicide among, 45, 52

Zealots, 14
Zeno of Citium, 113, 115, 117
Zilboorg, Gregory, 80
Zwingmann, Charles *("Krisentoleranz")*, 78

About the Author

Jacques Choron received his Ph.D. from Leipzig University, Germany, and his D.S.Sc. degree from the New School for Social Research in New York City. He is a distinguished philosopher, best known for his studies of the psychological and philosophical problems arising in connection with the phenomena of death. He is a long-time student of self-destructive phenomena. Most recently, he has been a Fellow at the Los Angeles Suicide Prevention Center and a Fellow at the Center for Studies of Suicide Prevention at the National Institute of Mental Health, Rockville, Maryland. Among his other books are *Death and Western Thought* and *Death and Modern Man* (originally published as *Modern Man and Mortality*).